REPORTING THE
GREAT WAR

REPORTING THE GREAT WAR

News from the Home Front

Stuart Hylton

Pen & Sword
MILITARY

First published in Great Britain in 2014 by
Pen & Sword Military
an imprint of
Pen & Sword Books Ltd
47 Church Street
Barnsley
South Yorkshire
S70 2AS

Copyright © Stuart Hylton 2014

ISBN 978 1 78346 357 2

A CIP catalogue record for this book is available from the British Library

Printed and bound in England by
CPI Group (UK) Ltd, Croydon, CR0 4YY

Pen & Sword Books Ltd incorporates the imprints of Pen & Sword Archaeology, Atlas, Aviation, Battleground, Discovery, Family History, History, Maritime, Military, Naval, Politics, Railways, Select, Social History, Transport, True Crime, and Claymore Press, Frontline Books, Leo Cooper, Praetorian Press, Remember When, Seaforth Publishing and Wharncliffe.

For a complete list of Pen & Sword titles please contact
PEN & SWORD BOOKS LIMITED
47 Church Street, Barnsley, South Yorkshire, S70 2AS, England
E-mail: enquiries@pen-and-sword.co.uk
Website: www.pen-and-sword.co.uk

Contents

PREFACE

When I wrote the Second World War counterpart to this book (*Reporting the Blitz*) I felt it necessary to give a word or two of explanation, as to why a further book was needed to complement the wealth of excellent written material on that part of our history. The same no doubt applies to this book.

Both books use local newspaper reports of the period as a major source. Whatever the shortcomings of provincial journalism (and there are plenty of those), the reports do help to capture a flavour of what it was like to live in that community through the war. A historian, applying their forensic analysis and the wisdom of hindsight, may give a more accurate account of events, but they do not necessarily capture a sense of how it felt to be there. Even the shortcomings – such as the omissions or distortions required by censorship or propaganda, or their inability to predict the future – are valuable in enabling us to share the immediate experience of the war to which the civilian population was exposed. We see, for example:

- how the authorities used patriotic fervour and hatred of the enemy as an aid to getting the whole of the population engaged in the war effort. Not for nothing was this thought of as the first total war;

- how the submarine blockade and the terror of bombing from the air brought the civilian population into the front line as never before;

- how other forms of new technology impinged on the war – from the internal combustion engine to the new horrors of warfare, like poison gas;

- how the business community tried to maintain 'business as usual', or better still to seek out the new opportunities for commerce that the war offered;

- how the authorities sought to control and use the new media – mass newspapers, cinema, wireless telegraphy – to ensure that it was their version of the war that got relayed to a better educated and more enfranchised public. This was also the first real propaganda war;

- how State control extended further and further into everybody's lives, with conscription, the blackout and rationing, along with the direction of labour, all anticipating the conditions of life more usually associated with the Second World War;

- how the war impacted on the role of women in society and, in particular, the labour market;

- how the idea of conscientious objection emerged alongside that of conscription, as a factor to be taken account of in recruitment;

- how the people tried to retain a sense of normality in what were extraordinary times, and life went on, in all its eccentric variety, despite everything.

As with the last book, I must disavow any claim for it being comprehensive or authoritatively accurate. What we are looking at is the first draft of history and, like all first drafts, it is prone to error. I have already referred to the dark hands of censorship and propaganda that coloured reports, and things that seem important to us now may have seemed much less so then (and vice versa). But each of these shortcomings is, in its own way, illuminating and I hope that this book will complement the wealth of other material now available about the home front in 1914–18. Think of it not so much as a history of the home front as an anthology of how it felt to be there.

I have to thank the many local history librarians and archivists up and down the country, who have without exception been most helpful to me in assembling the book. The photographs in it come either from the Imperial War Museum (prefixed IWM) or Reading Borough Council's Library Service, and the other illustrative material is taken from contemporary newspapers.

Chapter 1
A Quarrel in a Far-away Country

Few of us will forget the last week in the month (of July 1914), a week of calm and comfort when, under skies of Syrian blue, cloudless and serene, the hours passed dreamily away, and all things seemed to conspire to sooth us with the sense of security. It was true that some fears had arisen in the preceding weeks since a great tragedy had taken place at Serajevo; it was true that apprehensions had been aroused, but they had been lulled again; it was true that political seers had discerned ominous signs on the eastern horizon, but few could believe they were real portents of evil. Peace had so long prevailed, friendship had been so assiduously cultivated; goodwill to mankind had become so pure an aspiration, that the horror of a universal war seemed incredible and impossible.

Manchester City News
31 July 1915

On the 28 June 1914, the heir to the Austrian throne, Archduke Franz Ferdinand, and his wife were assassinated in Sarajevo by a 19-year-old Bosnian nationalist called Gavrilo Princip. Initially, the assassination passed virtually unnoticed in Britain. It seemed, as Neville Chamberlain was later to put it in a different context, like 'a quarrel in a far-away country between people of whom we know nothing'. To judge from the report of the event in one local paper, it should be seen primarily as a family tragedy for some distant set of foreign Royalty:

The murder of Archduke Franz Ferdinand and his wife, the Duchess of Hohenberg, adds yet another to the family afflictions and sorrows that have befallen the Royal House of Austria. No monarch has suffered so many tragic bereavements as the aged Emperor Franz Joseph.[1]

Franz Joseph had had his brother executed in Mexico, his wife assassinated and his only son was either murdered or committed suicide. Even more clear was that no one could foresee the enormous consequences of this deed. In their estimation, it should not lead even to a local war:

although Magyars, Czechs, Germans, Poles, Slavs and Russians may each have their grievances, they have none of them anything to gain from disruption, and if

Hungary separated from Austria she would straitway [sic] be at the mercy of Russia.²

When Prime Minister Asquith addressed the House of Commons about the assassination, he called it 'one of those incredible crimes that almost make us despair of the progress of mankind' and, according to one newspaper report, 'the tribute paid to the aged Francis Joseph was one of the noblest that has ever been delivered in Westminster and was worthy of the Prime Minister of a great and friendly nation'. Asquith praised the Emperor as 'the imperturbably sagacious and heroic head of a mighty state' and described the Austro-Hungarian Empire as 'rich in splendid traditions and associated in some of the most moving and treasured chapters of our common history'.³ Within weeks we would be at war with that Emperor, and that Empire.

Britain's great and good were certainly not letting events on the Continent interrupt the established round of society gatherings:

The season goes on quite gaily and there are no signs at present of an exodus from town. Last week was perhaps less conspicuous for the number of balls given, but probably Newmarket was the reason . . . London is likely to be lively until Goodwood, and certainly the town will not empty till well on into August, for a good many people return to town from Cowes before making a final departure either to the north or for a cure abroad.⁴

About the only disruption the society pages of the local papers initially had to report about the European crisis was that the Court Ball at Buckingham Palace had been postponed as a consequence of the assassination. Even as events on the Continent developed, it appeared to be royal business as usual. In the last week in July, just days before war broke out, the Palace flatly denied rumours that the situation would lead the Royal Household to abandon their habitual summer sojourn in Balmoral (a decision reversed during the first week of war). Only in the final days before war was there any indication of crisis in the Royal Household:

The breaking out of hostilities between Austria-Hungary and Servia, and the disturbed political situation at home, have seriously interfered with the King's plans, and in addition to his being absent from Goodwood races it is possible that the urgency of affairs may also prevent his attendance at Cowes Regatta and delay his northern shooting visits.⁵

One's view of the holiday situation for the common herd seemed to depend on which newspaper report you read. The very weekend that war broke out, the Cork Steamship Company was still advertising regular sailings to Antwerp, while Houlder Brothers could arrange five days in Belgium for £2 19*s* 6*d*, or a week on the Rhine for £6 10*s*. But were these Continental holidays being taken up?

There was a remarkable influx of holidaymakers at Blackpool today. Exactly 100 special trains ran in. Among visitors by train were many whose decision to visit continental resorts had been cancelled at the last moment.⁶

Another paper carried reports of disruption even to domestic holidays. What they described as 'seaside panic' had apparently set in, as holidaymakers in Britain made an early journey home in droves as war was declared. There was some suggestion that this was due to a fear of the German fleet shelling the British coast, a threat that the paper dismissed so long as the British fleet remained intact. They even cited the Hague Convention, which forbad the shelling of undefended towns, and criticised the early returners for their timidity:

> *Exodus from the seaside inflicts a double injury; it deprives those who live on the holiday-makers of their means of subsistence and it deprives the holiday-makers themselves of the health and vigour which to the children especially is so essential.[7]*

The Bournemouth Association of Hotels and Restaurants was equally concerned at this anxiety on the part of its customers and strove to reassure them:

> *The Bournemouth season was proceeding as usual, and the Association wish to emphasise that the misapprehension which exists that some of the Bournemouth hotels are, owing to the serious European trouble, unable to offer the usual comfort and attention, is entirely without foundation.[8]*

Just days before the declaration of war, the press was still of the view that it was a containable local dispute:

> *Grave as the news is from the Near East there is perhaps less reason for concern than at any time during the last three days of tension. The Standard publishes most important telegrams from Vienna and St Petersburg to the effect that the leading statesmen of the two nations are 'conversing in an amicable spirit'. Austria has already given a definite assurance that she desires no territorial expansion, and generally the exchange of views has been 'so satisfactory that the danger of a European war appears to be remote'. If Servia is 'not to be crushed' there will be no necessity for Russian interference, and if Russia does not move the general peace of Europe will not be disturbed.*
>
> *It is not difficult to see in this disposition of Austria to discuss the situation amicably with Russia, the hand of the Kaiser, whose boast it is that he helped keep the peace for a quarter of a century . . .[9]*

Some papers took a particularly partisan view of the declaration of war, when it came. One syndicated column even took the opportunity to provide some not entirely flattering pen portraits of leading Government figures in the House of Commons. These included someone who would one day become the darling of the Conservative party – the (then Liberal) First Lord of the Admiralty:

> *Mr Churchill, with all his courage, is one of the most high-strung men in political life. His cheeks were blotched with crimson and there was twitching of the lips. He laughed, and some men thought he was laughing at the likelihood of his appetite for fighting having much to feed upon; he laughed indeed, but I think it was the laugh of a man on the verge of hysteria.[10]*

They also took the opportunity to explore the reasons why the Kaiser so badly misjudged the national mood, which they garnished with a good dose of Jingoism:

> *the Kaiser and his advisors persuaded themselves that Great Britain was so*

bitterly divided politically and so seriously disturbed industrially that there was little prospect of her taking any effectual part in the conflict. The Germans completely failed to realise the fact that 'Britain in her hour of need is motherland the Empire through', and it would be interesting to secure the Kaiser's opinion of the most recent British 'political' development. This has taken the form of an agreement between the Unionist, Liberal and Labour parties to lend the full cooperation to the Government for the purpose of explaining the real causes of the war and its vital importance to the Kingdom, the Empire and indeed the whole world.[11]

About the only paper that seemed to have anticipated hostilities was the *Daily Mirror*, which, days before hostilities were declared and at a time when many still thought the crisis could be negotiated away, was promising 'exclusive war pictures'.

Most people in Britain were more interested in enjoying the weather. It had been a beautiful summer – ideal weather for garden parties. One such was organised by the Berkshire branch of the National Union of Women's Suffrage Societies. This was the 'respectable', polite face of the votes for women campaign, one of the hot political issues of the day. These were not the militant *suffragettes*, as the *Daily Mail* had chosen to christen them. In case anyone was in any doubt, one of the advertised attractions of the event was a talk by Mrs M. Jones on the virtues of law-abiding suffrage campaigning which would, she said, carry the day when other and less reputable methods had come to an end. The Newbury Conservative Party had its annual fete planned for the August Bank Holiday, but it found itself being overtaken by events:

Threatening clouds overshadowed the Conservative fete held in Shaw Avenue on Bank Holiday. Meteorologically it did not matter much, for although now and again the clouds discharged their showers, there was a sufficiency of sunshine, bright and cheerful, to allow of the holidaymakers getting all the enjoyment they desired out of the comprehensive programme provided. But there were tearful forebodings in the minds of all as to the outcome of the terrible complications in European affairs. The thought was uppermost, the expression readiest on the lips 'What is going to happen?' The news that came through was of the gravest character, and few, except the young and thoughtless, could find distraction in amusements, however alluring, or competitions, ever so exciting. The seriousness of the national situation had developed so rapidly that there was no question of abandoning the fete, as doubtless would have been done a few days later.

The elaborate programme was otherwise carried out in elaborate detail. Within a spacious ring there took place a series of sports, races for boys and girls, men and women, whippet racing and horse jumping. On the River Lambourn aquatic sports took place. Children danced in national and fancy costumes on the rectory lawn. In the grounds of Shaw House there was a contest of bands.[12]

There were signs of military activity all around the country, but not a lot that suggested we were preparing for war. In Cheshire, in the tradition of armies preparing for the re-run of their last war, rather than anticipating the forthcoming one, Boy Scouts re-enacted the relief of Mafeking. The village of Heaton Mersey was to play the part of the besieged town (with an invisible rampart all around it), defended by their local troop. Rival scouts were the besieging 'Boers', whose job it was to prevent the British Expeditionary Force (also known as the 10th Stockport Troop) from relieving the garrison. Each side wore a different coloured piece of wool around their forearms, and when that piece of wool was broken, you were officially 'dead'. Naturally the British won, 5–0 (by whatever means are used to score such events) and the losers graciously conceded that:

> *We were certainly inviting disaster in appointing ourselves 'Boers', as we might*
> *have known the British would come out victorious, as they usually do in*
> *difficulties.*[13]

Unlike the real Boer War, the rival armies spent the evening in the woods, enjoying 'tea and good fellowship' with their former 'enemies'. But the Boy Scouts were characteristically prepared for war, when it came. District Commissioners of the Scouts sent morale-boosting letters to each of their members:

> *You Boy Scouts of today, will remember your duty to your Country and your*
> *King. Whether God gives us quick victory, and honourable peace, or the war*
> *lasts long you will always be prepared to do your utmost to help . . . Boy Scouts*
> *ought to be more ready and more useful than most other boys, because you are fit*
> *in mind and body, because you are in training, because you have jolly times in*
> *camp and learn to use your wits, because you have all of you made your Scouts'*
> *promise.*[14]

In Swindon, the local authority took up the Boy Scouts' offer of support. They were given their own office in the town hall, from where they answered the Council's telephone outside office hours, delivered messages and performed other war service. In one area this included conducting a 'house to house visitation', to establish the whereabouts of enemy aliens, and at Worthing and elsewhere they performed coastguard duties. Their good work did not go unrecognised:

> *In future the 'BP [Baden Powell] hat' or Sea Scout cap and fleur de lys badge*
> *will be recognised by His Majesty's government as the uniform of a public*
> *service non-military body. This distinction is granted to the Boy Scout*
> *Association as a reward for the many public services which are being rendered*
> *by its members to the War Office and police authorities.*[15]

The Eton College contingent of the Officer Training Corps (no 'other ranks' training corps for Eton boys) was being inspected by Major General Davies, who took them to task for dirty boots (some of which appeared not to have been cleaned all week) and long hair. 'Long hair may be all right for men called "knuts"' he told them (knuts were the dandified fashion followers of the day) 'but it had nothing to do with soldiers. It made you look somewhere between a civilian and a foreigner.' At the other end of the age spectrum, a Reading hotel played host to a reunion of veterans of the Crimean War. The oldest participant was ex-Sergeant Melvin who, at the age of 81, had travelled up from

Portsmouth for the event. He had joined the Army as long ago as 1848 and had served in it for forty-four-and-a-half years.

There was not universal support for war. A body called the Neutrality League went so far as to place this full-page advertisement, opposing British involvement (which, unfortunately for them, appeared the day after war was declared):

> *Englishmen do your duty*
> *And keep your country out of a wicked and stupid war*
> *Small but powerful cliques are trying to rush you into it, but you must*
> *Destroy the plot today or it will be too late.*
> *Ask yourselves: why should we go to war?*

> *The war party say we must maintain the balance of power, because if Germany were to annex Belgium or Holland she would be so powerful as to threaten us; or because we are bound by treaty to fight for the neutrality of Belgium; or because we are bound by our agreements with France to fight for her.*
> *All these reasons are false. The War Party does not tell the truth.*

> 1. *If we took sides with Russia and France the balance of power would be upset like it never has been before. It would make the military Russian Empire of 160 million the dominant power in Europe. You know the kind of country Russia is.*

> 2. *We are not bound to join in a general European war to defend the neutrality of Belgium . . .*

> 3. *The Prime Minister and Sir Edward Grey have both emphatically and solemnly declared in the House of Commons that we have no undertaking whatever . . . to go to war for France.*

> 4. *If Germany did attempt to annex any part of Belgium, Holland or Normandy – and there is no reason to suppose she would attempt such a thing – she would be weaker than she is now, for she would have to use all her forces for holding her conquests down . . .*

> *It is your duty to save your country from this disaster.*
> *Act today or it may be too late.*[16]

Another distinguished voice – Bertrand Russell – spoke out against the war:

> *A month ago Europe was a peaceful group of nations; if an Englishman killed a German, he was hanged. Now, if an Englishman kills a German, he is a patriot. We scan the newspapers with greedy eyes for news of slaughter and rejoice when we read of innocent young men, blindly obedient to the word of command, mown down in thousands by the machine gun of Liege. Those who saw the London crowds, during the nights leading up to the declaration of war saw a whole population, hitherto peaceable and humane, precipitated in a few days down the steep slope to primitive barbarism, letting loose, in a moment, the instincts of hatred and bloodlust against which the whole fabric of society has been raised.*[17]

The real Army was at least recruiting, albeit nothing like on the scale they would shortly need. Their pre-war efforts seemed to focus on small advertisements like the one in this local paper:

His Majesty's Army

Young men are invited to join all branches of His Majesty's Army. Free food, housing, clothing, pay, education and medical attendance provided. Tradesmen receive a high rate of pay in the Royal Flying Corps and Royal Engineers. Every opportunity is given to well-conducted men to obtain promotion. Well-educated men can obtain a commission as an officer after three years' service in the ranks, with a grant of £150 to purchase uniform and £50 extra pay per annum for three years.[18]

Those wishing to become well educated enough to become an officer could apply to an address in Surrey for:

Thorough tuition, privately, in class or by post for the Army, Navy, universities, etc. by one of the MOST SUCCESSFUL teachers in the country . . . Recommended by the officers of the Life Guards. SUCCESS GUARANTEED.[19]

But recruitment was of no use if they could not retain the recruits:

A matter which is causing the authorities great anxiety is the great increase in the number of desertions from the army and of proof of this it may be mentioned that in 1905 896 men were lost to the Service in this way while this year so far 2,087 men have deserted.

And what might the causes of this be?

Excessive compulsion is considered by many of those who have the best opportunities of knowing to be largely responsible for this unsatisfactory state of affairs, and many commanding officers have yet to realise that they are dealing with a more highly educated, thinking and consequently more sensitive type of man than the soldier of a few years ago, and although discipline should not be allowed to relax one iota, the methods by which this discipline is taught and maintained must be altered to suit the type of men to whom it is to be applied.[20]

But the armed forces were not the only employers to offer overseas travel. The colonies were crying out for people to come and fill their empty spaces:

Lads! Lads! Lads!

To Australia for £3. The happiest healthiest life for British lads from 16 to 20 years is on big prosperous farms in New South Wales . . . Industrious farm boys may become substantial farmers.[21]

If you lacked the £3 fare to Australia, would-be domestic servants, typists and farm labourers could have their passage to Canada paid for them.

Domestic politics continued on its usual course right up to the outbreak of war. In the week before hostilities were declared, a local meeting at Newbury attracted a rising star of the left as its guest speaker:

Socialism was the subject of an address given by Mr Clement Attlee M.A., a university teacher, in the Market Place on Friday evening, though the greater part of the time was devoted to the question of wages, and he thought plenty before him didn't get more than 20 shillings a week . . . The trouble was the ever-widening depth between those who had too much and those who hadn't enough. What they had to do was to organise, send their own members to Parliament and support their own cause.[22]

THE BETTER WAY.

Drop that, man! You can do much better over there.

The war offers officially approved outlets for those with violent and destructive tendencies.

If world war was not on the minds of the people of Britain, the possibility of civil war certainly was. Ulstermen were known to have stockpiled 36,000 rifles and 2 million rounds of ammunition to stage an armed rising, should Ireland be granted Home Rule. This threat of internal strife was one of the factors that would lead Germany to assume (wrongly) that Britain would not wish to get involved in a Continental war. In the immediate run-up to the declaration of war, it was the Irish question that still held centre stage. The headlines in the local papers in the very week before the declaration of war referred to the King and the crisis – but the crisis they were referring to was the Irish one:

The gracious and timely suggestion made by his Majesty has afforded an additional and final opportunity to secure a peaceful settlement of the Irish crisis, and it is to be hoped that it will be utilised in the best, most effective and most prompt manner possible.[23]

When it came, the declaration of war brought out people's patriotic instincts:

Extraordinary themes of enthusiasm were witnessed in London on Tuesday night.

The enthusiasm culminated outside Buckingham Palace. A lady came out of the Palace and announced that war had been declared. This was received with tremendous cheering, which grew to a deafening roar when King George, Queen Mary and the Prince of Wales appeared on the balcony shortly after 11 o' clock . . .

As if by general accord, the cheers gave way to the singing of the National Anthem, which was taken up lustily by the whole throng.

For fully five minutes the Royal party remained on the balcony. They retired amidst a perfect storm of cheering and although the crowd subsequently began to melt away, thousands remained.[24]

With excursion bookings cancelled, Londoners were forced in many cases to spend Bank Holiday in the Metropolis, and, indeed, so great was the obsession of the popular mind with the European agitation that many felt small disposition to retreat to the country. The neighbourhood of Parliament Square and Buckingham Palace presented a remarkable experience. Crowds cheered taxi cabs on the chance of somebody of importance being inside, and when, occasionally a leading personality was indubitably recognised the enthusiasm was boisterous. Many of the demonstrators wore small Union Jacks on their coats and hats, accompanied in some cases by the Tricolour. In and out among the crowd walked the advocates of neutrality, exhorting the public by handbill and sandwich board to insist that England should 'stand clear'.[25]

In contrast to this cheerful patriotism, there were tearful – not to say hysterical – scenes at Victoria station, as French reservists embarked for home. The 'Marseillaise' was sung and tears were streaming down the cheeks of the women seeing their loved ones off. Several fainted and had to be carried off the platform. There was one woman in widow's weeds 'whose shrieks pierced the entire expanse of the station' as she ran down the platform alongside the departing train. The British at Waterloo station were naturally more controlled:

At the great London railway terminus, there were almost unprecedented scenes of patriotism, not unmingled with pathos, at the parting of husbands and wives, fathers and children.[26]

In a separate display of patriotism, a crowd gathered outside the German Embassy in London and expressed its justifiable anger by breaking the windows, until the police were called in. When something similar happened in St Petersburg, the papers called it 'mob rule'. Just as well that the German Embassy protesters were not there at the same time as those expatriate German nationalists who sang 'Deutschland Uber Alles' outside it, as their Ambassador left for the homeland. This paper took it as a credit to the British that the singers were allowed to depart unscathed:

> *No patriotic Englishman will regret that the audacity of the singers proved so inexpensive to them; on the contrary. Nothing could be much more undesirable in England just now than an anti-German feeling, and nothing more irrational. It cannot be too clearly insisted that our quarrel is not with the German people – a great nation, groaning under the weight of a despotism which, grown mad in these days with the lust of power seems bent on committing suicide before the eyes of Europe.[27]*

From the outset, the Government was concerned to avoid panic over food supplies and, within days of the declaration, the President of the Board of Agriculture issued this reassurance:

> *The supply of wheat at present in this country, together with the home crops now being harvested, is sufficient for four months ordinary consumption . . . Large consignments of wheat are now on the way to this country and much of it is, in fact, close to our shores . . .*
>
> *The situation with regard to meat is not less satisfactory. The normal killings of our home-grown stock supply 60 per cent of our annual consumption. We are not necessarily dependent on foreign imports for the balance of our supplies . . . There is, therefore, no justification in the present position for any rise in price in bread or meat.[28]*

Even so, some of the first people to feel the effects of the war were housewives, as they shopped:

> *As a result of the war cables, prices of provisions are rising in all parts of the country. The price of a quartern loaf will, it is announced, go up a halfpenny in London next Tuesday, and it is not to be supposed that the provinces will escape an equal, if not greater, increase. Enquiries made last night from a well-known Reading provision merchant yielded the information that at present the war had made very little difference to local retail prices.*
>
> *'But,' added our informant, 'It is bound to do so in a very short time. You cannot buy any sugar at the present time,' he said 'or even get an offer. One of the biggest men in the London trade did not open up his premises at all today and another, after putting up his prices, shut up after ten minutes. Sugar will be affected as much or more than anything. Flour is anything from 2s to 5s dearer, wheat went up again today and the prices of bacon, butter and foreign eggs are all affected. The increase in the price of bacon was stated to be nearly 1s 2d a pound.[29]*

One Liverpool retailer had inflated the prices of his wares, allegedly in an attempt to protect supplies to those regular customers to whom they were contracted. But it was to no avail; it appeared that there were panic-stricken customers who were prepared to stockpile foodstuffs at almost any price. Once the initial rush had died down, the retailer offered the panic-stricken the opportunity to repent of their ways:

THE RING.

High bread prices in 1915 lead to allegations of price-fixing by farmers or bakers.

> *Now that the public realise their fears of a food famine were groundless, we are prepared to take back superfluous stocks. All who purchased at panic prices can, if they desire, return the goods to us. Purchase money will be refunded, or credit notes issued.[30]*

Their cause can hardly have been helped by a rival store stating in the same edition of the paper:

> *for the moment prices cannot be much reduced. This refers particularly to butter, bacon, ham, cheese, lard, eggs, flour, cereals and meat goods.[31]*

If the outbreak of war led to panic buying, it also prompted a potential run on the £ and an outbreak of panic weddings. The Bank Holiday was extended by a further three days, to try and prevent the former, until people calmed down, but the rush into wedlock lasted rather longer:

> *So many Army and Navy officers are applying for special marriage licences that in order to facilitate the issue of such business arrangements have been made for*

the Faculty Office, Knightrider Street, to remain open continuously both day and night for the next few days.[32]

Military people were immediately mobilised, and few can have been less happy about it than one George Blakeman, who received his recall to his regiment while en route from his wedding reception to his honeymoon destination. The papers were at pains to tell their readers what a fine-looking bunch of people our armed forces were:

Comment was made on every hand on the orderly and sober appearance of the general body of the men. The recent training they had received had evidently not been forgotten and with uniform step and erect of carriage, the lines of sailors went their way to the barracks . . . Nothing in the way of a war scare, however gloomy the outlook, appeared to have the effect of dampening the spirits of 'the Jolly Tar'.

As for the Royal Navy Reserves, mostly fishermen who had been called up to replace trawling for herrings by fishing for mines, they were:

Fine specimens of sea-hardened manhood . . .[33]

For those left behind, this local paper set about its self-appointed task of putting the community onto a war footing:

England expects every man to do his duty

Yes, every man! Not merely those who are in the fighting rank, but those also who stay at home. How can we do our duty to our country in a time of crisis as serious as that which closed at Waterloo? There is a strong temptation at such a time to take the position of a spectator at a thrilling drama . . . But mere excitement that is not productive of any action is not only useless but positively injurious to character; it is as bad as a debauch of sentimentalism through constant doses of highly-spiced fiction . . . What can we do? In the first place we can resolve to do our ordinary work as well and as quietly as possible. Time must not be wasted in rushing about for war news and chattering about every sensational item that is published . . . Next to doing the daily work there will certainly be some special bit of work for the country which we can do; for most of us, it will be in the form of contributing to the relief of those whose breadwinners have gone to serve their country and then also to the help of those whom the war throws out of work and brings their wives and families to destitution. There is active bodily service for those who can give it. Young men are needed, young unmarried men, to rally round the flag and enlist in the ranks of the army . . . Those who employ Reservists and Territorials have their opportunity in dealing generously with them, continuing as much of their pay as they can afford, and keeping their places open for them. Employers and employed should bring their disputes to an end . . . Finally, as the last and greatest of the active positive duties we need mention, is that of prayer and intercession.[34]

One scoutmaster, apparently part of the Territorial reserve, wrote to his local paper as he travelled back to his unit to be mobilised:

> *The war promises to be terrible in all respects, and fearful hardship and*
> *suffering will no doubt be experienced before we again have peace . . . Hundreds*
> *will pay the penalty of their loyalty with their lives.*[35]

Leaving aside for a moment his wild under-estimate of the scale of casualties the war would bring, his main purpose in writing to the press seemed to be to scotch rumours that there was to be a wholesale conscription of Boy Scouts. (Early in the war, H.G. Wells proposed putting together a rag-tag army of those hitherto considered too old or unfit to fight, Boy Scouts and others, to supplement the regular forces.) The Boy Scouts were a peace movement, our correspondent pointed out (though, if Mafekin needed relieving again, the 10th Stockport Scouts might no doubt offer the experience of their recent exercise to the cause).

Even miscreants found themselves swept up in the patriotic fervour. George Barry had enjoyed a rather extended (and unofficial) spell of leave from the Army, having deserted in 1897. After almost twenty years on the run, he surrendered himself at the police station, hoping to be re-united with his regiment and have a crack at the enemy. He was one of many deserters up and down the country who suddenly re-discovered their enthusiasm for military life. The Government eventually granted them a conditional amnesty, if they returned to the fold by 4 September.

Communities were desperate for the latest news of the war. In the days before electronic communications, this meant primarily the newspapers. At Henley, anxious

In the days before radio and television, newspapers were just about the only source of war news.

During the War
'Phone 91x
is at your service

WAR!   WAR!

During the War
'Phone 91x
is at your service

J. TUFNAIL, Newsagent, Newbury

(WHOLESALE AND RETAIL),

WILL BE OPEN FROM SEVEN A.M. TO TEN P.M. DURING THE WAR.

J. TUFNAIL is Agent for all the MORNING and EVENING PAPERS, including Times, Standard, Morning Post, Telegraph, Daily Graphic, Mail, Mirror, Express, Chronicle, Daily News and Sketch.

DAILY EVENING PAPERS SUPPLIED BY POST.

All SPECIAL NEWS is trained at the earliest possible moment to J. TUFNAIL after the receipt of Telegrams and 'Phone announcements. Latest 'Phone is received Nightly at 9 p.m., which is shown on Window.

SUNDAY and FOLLOWING SUNDAYS during the War on Sale from EIGHT a.m., **Times and other Dailies when published ;** Also The People, Lloyds, News of the World, Dispatch, Reynolds, Referee, Observer, Sunday Times, etc.

All interested in the War (Customers or not) Our War 'Phone is at your service.

crowds gathered at the railway station, awaiting the arrival of *The Times* or the *Daily Mail*. So dense did they get that the police were brought in to control them, and access to the station had to be banned to all but rail travellers. The rest were disappointed when the train pulled in with news that all the newspapers had been snapped up in London.

Radio was by now established as a medium of communication, if not yet of entertainment or public information (Marconi had transmitted his first transatlantic message as long ago as 1901, but the BBC was still a decade in the future). With war, came an appreciation of its potential for espionage. Edward Tunbridge was an early enthusiast for wireless telegraphy, and one of his favourite activities was to listen to, and communicate with, the broadcasts from the communications centre established on the Eiffel Tower. With the coming of the war, he was aware of a lot of mysterious coded traffic coming from that source. The next thing he noticed was the banging on his front door, as the man from the post office arrived to shut his equipment down for the duration.

It was the cause of Belgian neutrality that finally dictated British involvement. But were the German people really behind their leaders' belligerence, or was it just the work of a militaristic elite? A correspondent, identified only as 'AS', offered the newspapers the benefit of his (self-appointed) expert knowledge of Germany and the Germans:

> *Neither the commercial nor the working classes have desired war. They have shrunk from it, not on principle but for practical reasons, because it would disturb their comfort. And they are in general quite friendly towards Englishmen . . . But underneath this peaceable and friendly surface lies a deep and general animosity towards England. There is no class in Germany that would not rejoice at her humiliation . . . It is not individual Englishmen that Germans dislike, but England as a power. At the same time they despise her, as they do all other nations except the Americans, whom they fear as commercial rivals. They believe that England is played out industrially, commercially, politically and even nautically – in a military sense she has long ceased to count – and they yearn to seize her heritage, provided that it can be done at small cost.[36]*

But this would be a war in which nothing would be seized at small cost.

Chapter 2
Terror from the Air

If what we do is frightful, then may frightfulness be Germany's salvation.

Peter Strasser, Commander of the German Zeppelin fleet

It is far better to face the bullets than to be killed at home by a bomb. Join the army at once and help to stop an air raid.

War Office recruitment poster

A woman in London says she doesn't mind the air raids, since they take her mind off the war.

Joke © 1918

Britain before the war

This war would be the first to use aerial bombing to bring civilian populations into the front line. Britain's attitude to aerial warfare in the years before 1914 was, to put it mildly, ambivalent. The Hague Peace Convention of 1899 sought an agreement to ban 'the dropping of projectiles or explosives from balloons or other airships'. The only government to refuse to sign it was Britain, who declined on the grounds that that the employment of such a tactic would give a huge advantage to a country like Britain, with only a small standing army. Not until 1907 did they become a signatory to a revised treaty.

At the same time, there was a deep scepticism within the British armed forces (partly born of rival vested interests) about the military value of flying machines. In 1908 the Minister of War was advised by his Parliamentary Private Secretary, Colonel J.E.B. Seely, that 'we do not consider that aeroplanes will be of any possible use for war purposes', and Sir William Nicholson, the Chief of General Staff between 1908 and 1912, described aviation as 'a useless and expensive fad advocated by a few individuals whose ideas are unworthy of attention'. The *Manchester Guardian* agreed, saying in an editorial that 'we cannot understand to what practical use a flying machine that is heavier than air can be put'.[1]

Even the leadership of the Royal Flying Corps, formed in 1912, had a very blinkered view of aviation's potential. Brigadier General David Henderson, the head of the RFC's Military Wing, took the view that Germany would not bomb 'undefended towns . . . no enemy would risk the odium such action would involve'. In his view, the only role for the aeroplane in warfare was reconnaissance. This led the designers at the Royal Aircraft Factory at Farnborough down a hopelessly blind avenue. Accurate reconnaissance, it was argued, required slow flying, so in 1913, the RFC was limited to developing planes with engines of less than 100hp. Pilots were told to remove any home-made armaments they had fitted to their craft, and were actively discouraged from practising the aerobatics that could be their best hope of getting out of trouble, if engaged in combat. The net result of this, at the outbreak of war, was that the RFC had few aircraft with the performance to catch even Zeppelins, no way of attacking them, even if they could catch them, and no way of responding to any challenge to their own aircraft.

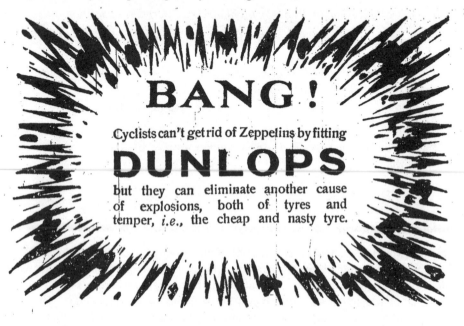

**Dunlops latch onto the current preoccupation with Zeppelins
to promote their product.**

But even their reconnaissance role was disputed by some at the very top of the chain of command. Despite his forces having been soundly defeated in a 1912 military exercise by opponents who used aerial reconnaissance, Douglas Haig, no less, felt able to advise a group of his officers in 1914:

> *I hope none of you gentlemen is so foolish as to think that aeroplanes will be usefully employed for reconnaissance purposes in the air. There is only one way for a commander to get information by reconnaissance, and that is by the use of cavalry.*[2]

The war was barely a month old, and Britain had not yet experienced bombing, when this local paper reassessed the threats posed by the airship and the aeroplane:

> *The Great War will put many theories to the proof, among others the views held*

as to the relative value of airships and aeroplanes, and the part they are fitted to play in war. For offence it has not yet been shown that either one or the other is of much value. The aeroplanes on the other hand, have done much splendid work in scouting; they have been the eyes of the armies on both sides. Our own Royal Flying Corps has been repeatedly mentioned as having secured the mastery of the air. As to the Zeppelins, it has yet to be shown that their destructive powers are of any use from the military point of view. They have destroyed some buildings and taken the lives of a few civilians in Antwerp and Brussels, that is all. Those that think that London can be seriously threatened by airships may find some difficulty in explaining why Paris has escaped destruction . . . Nevertheless, it would not be an extravagant precaution if the Government were to provide Oxford and Cambridge with searchlights and such guns as are effective against aircraft.[3]

This last reference, to Oxford and Cambridge, follows the Germans' destruction of Louvain, a university town sometimes described as the Belgian Oxford.

But this complacency was not shared by the entire public. In his 1908 book *The War in the Air*, science fiction writer H.G. Wells imagined the flying machines of the future wreaking havoc on New York, and the *Daily Mail* ran an alarmist campaign about the danger. A widely shown 1911 film, showing a city from the control car of a Zeppelin and emphasising how vulnerable that city would be to attack, led to an *airship panic*, and to many false sightings of Zeppelins over Britain. But British interests had their own plans for airships. Just days before the outbreak of war, the Britannia Airship Committee announced plans for a British-made airship that would carry seventy-five passengers and fifteen crew across the Atlantic at 60 miles an hour. All they needed was someone to finance it.

But if real-life evidence of the potential of the flying machine was needed at the outset of the war, it could be found in the newspapers in July 1914. A former Royal Navy Lieutenant, John Cyrill Porte, announced his plan to fly across the Atlantic, and this local newspaper was left breathless in admiration:

The amazing achievements of the past few years have almost robbed us of the capacity for wonder at anything new in the domain of human ingenuity and intrepidity [sic]. Nevertheless, the prospect of flying from America to Europe is so daring an adventure that it is impossible to read about Lieutenant Porte's preparations for his Atlantic flight without a feeling of astonishment . . . But Lieutenant Porte has no misgivings. He is confident that, barring accidents, the feat can be accomplished and he is leaving nothing to chance in his arrangements.[4]

In the event, Porte's flight had to be abandoned because of the onset of war, and his death from tuberculosis in 1919 prevented him pursuing his dream after it.

Thrills and spills

The potential for aerial warfare was there, but the fact that aviation was still in its infancy meant that crashes like the following were commonplace:

*Much excitement was caused in the Palmer Park, Reading, on Christmas day,
where an aeroplane came in contact with the top of a tree. On the previous day
two airmen descended into the park, owing to the strand wires of one of the
machines breaking. The machine was repaired, and next morning the airman
pushed it over to near the London Road entrance in order to have a clean sweep
in ascending. Immediately he did so it was apparent that something was amiss.
The altitude first of all was extremely low. The aeroplane proceeded along near
to St Bartholomew's Road, swerved around and then, narrowly missing
Councillor Eighteen's house in the Wokingham Road, came back and struck the
top of a small lime tree near to the Wokingham Road, so that it fell with a crash
to the ground. Fortunately the airman jumped from the machine in time, and so
escaped injury. The machine was afterwards taken away on a lorry.[5]*

Air accidents could also have their ghoulish side, and in February 1918 a plane crashed
near Basingstoke, killing both crew:

*Within a few minutes of the disaster a number of boys just released from school
rushed to the spot but were kept at a distance until the bodies of the unfortunate
airmen had been removed. After this, the boys and a number of soldiers
assembled about the machine, certain valuable parts of which, besides others of
lower account, were taken away.[6]*

Wreckage or not, it was still Government wreckage and the authorities tracked down and
prosecuted the boys responsible. Their defence, that they had been given the parts by the
soldiers, did not impress the magistrates and they were fined 10s each.

First World War military aircraft were not just dangerous to the people who flew them,
or who lived beneath their bombing runs; they could even be a hazard to the people who
designed them. One such was 22-year-old Edwin Boyle:

*An aeronautical enthusiast since the age of twelve, Boyle had recently been
assisting to perfect a contrivance whereby pilots and observers might safely land
from a machine while in flight should an accident occur in mid-air.[7]*

Or, as we might call it, a parachute. The Air Board had consistently refused to issue such
devices to the aircrews, since:

*The presence of such apparatus might impair the fighting spirit of pilots and
cause them to abandon machines which might otherwise be capable of returning
to base for repair.[8]*

The account of Mr Boyle's contribution to aeronautical research continued:

*Captain Arthur Payne, Flight Commander RAF, went up with Boyle in an
aeroplane for experimental purposes. At a height of 400 feet he told Boyle to get
out on the wing and sit on the specially-constructed platform. He had not done
that before, as it was the first descent Boyle had attempted.*

*'When we got to the right position' said Captain Payne 'I gave him the signal
to let go. He went over the side in the ordinary way, but the parachute casing
gave way with the parachute, instead of remaining on the machine. This was*

caused by the breaking of a hook, and Boyle fell to the ground and was instantly killed.'[9]

The war comes to British skies

By contrast to Britain's ambivalence, flying machines had been part of real-life German military planning since the start of the century. The Schlieffen Plan, the Germans' 1905 master strategy for fighting a European war, had envisaged a real aerial bombardment of Britain as a precursor to any invasion. Under the plan, once their forces had advanced as far as Calais, London would be within a hundred miles of them. They even had a force – the quaintly named *Brieftauben Abteilung Ostende* (BAO – or Ostend Carrier Pigeon Department) – ear-marked to carry out the bombardment. In the event, the German offensive bogged down east of Calais, leaving London out of the range of the aircraft of the day. It would be 1917, when their Gotha bombers started coming into service, before aircraft could (just) threaten London from inside German lines. However, by 1914 the Germans had already developed military Zeppelins that could travel at 136kph, climb to 4,250m and carry a 2,000kg payload of bombs. They *could* reach London. But not even every German military man was convinced of their value, as this German staff officer, taken prisoner of war, told his captors:

There is not a naval or military officer of standing who really believes in zeppelins . . . But because the Emperor has set his mind on them nobody has dared say what he really thought, and in consequence immense sums, which could have been more appropriately spent, were paid for experiments, construction and for hangers. My own opinion – the opinion of 99 staff officers out of 100 – is that they are nothing more or less than a swindle, foisted on our Emperor by a silly old man [Count Zeppelin].[10]

The reality of aerial warfare became evident within days of the outbreak of war. The French authorities seemed rather more alive to the danger, and immediately put a string of strong searchlights along its eastern borders. However, they seemed to have little more idea of how to deal with the Zeppelin threat than Britain did:

Grim and desperate instructions have been given to aviators to cope with this sudden danger. Directly, it is stated, the German air fleet is sighted, seven aviators will at once engage them. Their plan is to fly over the dirigibles and attempt to wreck them with special projectiles. Should this fail . . . the aviators must charge the enemy and attempt to rent the envelope. This is a forlorn hope, and if it is to be taken, will certainly mean the death of the aviator piloting the charging machine.[11]

Sure enough, Paris was bombed on 13 August 1914 and Antwerp suffered no less than 800kg of bombs, dropped from two Zeppelins, on the 26 August. This threw into harsh relief the inadequacy (not to say almost total absence) of aerial defence at home. Inland Britain was at this time protected by just one Vickers Gunbus, and a handful of other aircraft considered too obsolete to go with the British Expeditionary Force to France. These latter tended to be too slow and unable to climb fast enough even to engage with the Zeppelins, always assuming they were alerted soon enough to give them a sporting chance of making contact (which was by no means always the case). The few individual pilots who managed to engage with the enemy found themselves isolated and outgunned. Most of the ground-based guns available for anti-aircraft duty could not elevate their barrels far enough to hit an aircraft and, in any event, the head of home defence Sir John French issued the extraordinary order that, for some reason, guns should not fire on aircraft 'even if recognised as hostile'. This was not rescinded until June 1917. Nor was the potential of ground-to-air radio exploited; the Navy banned its use, lest it interfere with naval signals traffic.

In the coastal areas, the Royal Naval Air Service (a separate wing, controlled by the Royal Navy) fared rather better, with some seventy-one aircraft available to protect them. From 3 September 1914, Kitchener put the Royal Navy in sole charge of Britain's home air defences. (They later had to hand it back to the Royal Flying Corps, as their aircraft became more than fully committed in trying to deal with the submarine menace.)

Before any aerial attacks took place, British civilians found themselves in the front line for the very first time, when Whitby, Scarborough and Hartlepool were hit by German naval gunfire in December 1914. The raid on Hartlepool stimulated a huge demand for souvenir pieces of shrapnel. Not even the director of the local museum was able to get a piece to exhibit, despite having had a shell go through the roof of his own library. A worker doing a job on the site at the time made off with the souvenirs. When supplies of the real thing ran out, some enterprising locals took to manufacturing 'shrapnel' to meet demand. One of them claimed to have made £300 from these souvenirs.

It is generally held that Britain's first taste of aerial warfare came on 19 January 1915, when two Zeppelins attacked Great Yarmouth, Kings Lynn and Sheringham. But Britain actually ceased to be an island for military purposes on Christmas Eve, 1914, when a sole German seaplane, flying at the very limit of its range, dropped a single bomb on a garden in Dover, destroying some Brussels sprouts and breaking a few windows. By the standards of the bombing that was to come, even the January Zeppelin raid on East Anglia was a relatively minor affair – twenty-four 50kg bombs and some incendiaries were dropped, four people were killed and sixteen injured.

On 10 May 1915 Southend was the victim of an early Zeppelin attack, in which a 60-year-old female member of the Salvation Army was killed and £20,000 of damage was caused. Suspiciously, a large quantity of wood was set alight on Southend cliffs, near the site of the raid, shortly beforehand. Local opinion held that the Germans had targeted particular buildings, like the electricity works, though the reality was that the Zeppelins often struggled to know which county, let alone which building, was beneath them. The Germans dropped more than bombs:

> *The following message, written on a piece of cardboard in blue pencil, was found the garden of 11, Rayleigh Avenue, Southend, having evidently been attached to a bomb: 'You English. We have come, and we'll come again soon. Kill or cure. German'.* [12]

One thing the raid singularly failed to do was to terrorise the local population:

> *A party of girls was hurrying along the Leigh front towards Southend in pursuit*

*of the Zeppelin. One lagged a little behind, and her companions shouted out
'Come along, do hurry, or you will miss the fun!'*[13]

The bomb damage immediately attracted ghoulish sightseers in great numbers, some of
whom barely troubled to change out of their night attire, and many of whom, the paper
noted disapprovingly, were 'without collar and tie':

> *After six, when the trams started, they brought up hundreds of sight-seers. Others
> came in by trap, by cycle, afoot, in motors from the surrounding countryside. The
> streets soon looked like a Sunday midday.*[14]

The raid did, however, raise a number of questions as the community reflected upon it.
Were our defences adequate?

> *Where, say Leigh folk, were our aircraft and air guns? Are we to be exposed to
> this kind of thing indefinitely, without any hope of protection? These are
> questions which are quite natural, and it is hoped that, even if no answer is
> vouchsafed for military reasons, the next visit of the German airships will meet a
> vigorous and warm reception.*[15]

It also prompted a journalistic review of the local fire service. Were its resources (one
fire engine, one fire escape, 2,000ft of hose and sixteen full-time and twenty part-time
firemen) adequate to cope with the new incendiary menace? (In this raid they had had to
contend with eleven fires simultaneously.) They called for members of the police force
to be trained to supplement them, where necessary, and to be given their own hoses.
Finally, the raid led to violent riots against Germans and German property in the town.
This resulted in two-hundred special constables and the Army being called in to restore
order. Despite considerable damage and disorder, only two of the rioters were ever
arrested.

At first, the Kaiser withheld permission to bomb London, being unwilling to put its
historic monuments (as distinct from its people) at risk, and fearful of the effect of such
an indiscriminate weapon upon neutral opinion. However, he gradually succumbed to
military pressure and, on 31 May 1915, the first Zeppelin attack on the capital took place.
It dropped eighty-seven incendiaries and twenty-five high-explosive bombs, though the
Admiralty communiqué issued after the raid seemed to cast doubt on whether it had
really happened:

> *Zeppelins are reported to have been seen near Ramsgate and Brentford, and in
> certain outlying parts of London. Many fires are reported, but these cannot
> absolutely be connected with the visit of airships.*[16]

This communiqué was greeted sceptically by the public, and contributed to a general
mistrust of future official pronouncements. By the time the Government decided to go
public with the full story, the damage to their reputation had been done. If their intention
was to keep the location of the attack secret from German intelligence, their behaviour
was even more inexplicable, since German newspapers identified the areas bombed from
the outset. The Government's policy of news management nonetheless prevailed, and
when Sheerness was attacked in June, all the local paper for the area was allowed to refer
to was the bombing of *a* 'Kentish town'. The press were given stern warnings against

reporting virtually anything about air raids (though that did not stop them publishing the stern warning itself, so the public at least knew the limits under which the press laboured):

> *The press are specifically reminded that no statement whatever must be published dealing with the places in the neighbourhood of London reached by aircraft, or the course proposed to be taken by them, or any statement or diagram which might indicate the ground or route covered by them. The Admiralty communiqué is all the news which can properly be published.*[17]

The public and the air war

By the end of the war, some 1,413 British civilians would have lost their lives in 51 air raids. Most public opinion was outraged by this new escalation of modern warfare. There were calls in Parliament and elsewhere for pre-emptive strikes against German air-force targets and for reprisal raids on German cities. The *Daily Mail* published a reprisals map, showing all the German cities within bomber range of the Allied front line and inquest juries recorded verdicts of wilful murder against the Kaiser and his son. Former First Sea Lord John Fisher went one stage further, calling for German nationals in Britain to be taken hostage, with one of them being shot for every Briton killed in air raids. The random and civilian nature of the bombing casualties quickly earned the Zeppelins the nickname of 'baby killers'. It was even claimed that, in the early raid on Antwerp, they were using unsporting bombs:

> *It is officially stated that the projectiles used were different from those used on the former occasion. They were filled with special bullets calculated to inflict horrible wounds. Such a type of bomb has never been used by artillery, and is completely unknown to them.*[18]

This editor was in no doubt as to the correct response to air raids:

> *It is idle to pretend that the nation should submit calmly to such treatment and should hesitate to give the German people a dose of the same physic, because of a feeling against reprisals. The German government represent these raids to their people as the marvellous achievements of their aviators . . . If the enemy persists in waging warfare from the air against this country, it is obvious that the only policy is to hit back harder and harder until the enemy has had enough . . . to bring home to the German people what raids mean to the civilian population is not reprisal, but prevention . . . An offensive policy is always the cheapest and the most effective. To be merely on the defensive means that thousands of aeroplanes, guns and men must be employed to repel the attacks of a few planes . . . It did not take a great deal of imagination to foresee the development of the aeroplane and air warfare, and we ought to have been not only ready, but dealing the Germans effective blows . . . With the great resources of America as well as our own, and that of our allies, it should be quite easy to beat the Germans out of the air presently.*[19]

Not everybody favoured reprisals:

> *We have today the verdict of the civilised peoples of the world on our side; and*

politically and ethically it would be sheer unwisdom to make ourselves unfit to teach Germany the lessons she will have to learn before the restoration of peace to Europe.[20]

The Allied bombing strategy, by contrast, was a positive master class in sportsmanship. Readers were told that, for Allied flyers:

Instructions are always issued to confine the attacks to points of military importance and every effort is made to avoid dropping bombs on any residential portions of the towns.[21]

But not everyone in Britain seemed to be equally outraged by the idea of bombing. In what seems like an extraordinary gift to German propagandists, prominent peer Lord Montagu said:

The Germans have a perfect right to raid London. It is defended by guns and squadrons of aeroplanes and it is the chief seat of energy for the war. We are only deluding ourselves when we talk about London being an undefended city, and of no military importance.[22]

Accordingly, future German propaganda relating to the bombing of London generally referred to it as *the fortified city*. Lord Derby, the War Minister, also went against the grain of public opinion when he said:

It would be better to be defeated, retaining honour, chivalry and humanity, rather than obtain a victory by methods which have brought upon Germany universal execration.[23]

During 1915 and the early part of 1916 the Zeppelins were virtually untouched by the British defences. They flew at 10,000ft, out of reach of British gunfire (had they been firing) and, by the time the Allied fighters of the day had climbed up to meet them, they would be long gone. But gradually a new generation of higher performance aircraft and new anti-Zeppelin munitions (a cocktail of soft-headed, high-explosive and incendiary bullets designed to set fire to them) put the defenders at an advantage.

The shooting down of a Zeppelin in September 1916 was invested with huge significance by parts of the press:

The fall of the blazing airship near Enfield is symbolical of nothing less than the final ruin of the central powers.[24]

The same report described its last moments in colourful terms:

Suddenly, away further to the north a ball of fire in the sky riveted our attention, and then suddenly there was a great explosion. The whole of London, north, south, east and west, was illuminated by that one awful flash. The dome of St Pauls and the towers at Westminster, hitherto obscured to our view, stood out with remarkable clearness and for a brief moment it looked as if a panoramic view of the whole of London had been thrown upon a screen in a darkened hall.[25]

It was said that the fire of the stricken Zeppelin could be seen 40 miles away, and the village of Cuffley where it fell became a place of pilgrimage for hordes of sightseers and souvenir hunters. The pilot who carried out the deed was given the VC and his aeroplane was put on public exhibition. If the Royal Flying Corps needed further incentive, the proprietor of the *Newcastle Daily Chronicle* had in February 1916 offered a £1,000 prize to the crew of the first aircraft to shoot down a Zeppelin. Attempts to build higher performance German airships were not successful, and the shooting down of two Zeppelins in one day (28 November 1916) effectively marked the end of their war.

That same day also saw the first raid on London by Gotha bombers. Even these were at the limit of their range, but they were at least as fast as some of the ageing fighters pursuing them, and had about the same operational ceiling. They tended to be much more at risk from their unreliable Mercedes engines than they were from Britain's air defences.

By 1916 the lack of coordination between the Royal Flying Corps and the Royal Naval Air Service was persuading many of the need for change. Lord Montagu spoke on the subject to a meeting of the South Buckinghamshire Conservative Association. The two services were failing to cooperate, even to the point of competing with each other to buy the same equipment. They also cut across each other in specifying the aircraft they bought, trying to get the same aeroplanes to do bombing, fighting, reconnaissance and aerial photography, when they should have been developing purpose-built machines for each role. The time was fast approaching when the two should be merged into a free-standing third arm of the services, with its own executive. Montagu called this new force the Imperial Air Service, but when it finally emerged in April 1918 it was named the Royal Air Force.

Raids on the south-east coast involving two pairs of German planes in February 1916 highlighted the shambolic state of Britain's air defences – at least, if the account of it given in the Commons by Mr Bennett-Goldney, Unionist MP for Canterbury, were to be believed:

'I have just come from a district where there has been another daylight raid' he said 'and, as on previous occasions, the enemy aircraft left our shores unscathed.

'A month ago when a previous raid took place, the machines were not ready and the officers were not present. What happened? A battle between one of our aeroplanes and one of our seaplanes, both of which mistook the other for the enemy.

'But even that is not enough, for, having witnessed the fray, our anti-aircraft gunners turned their fire on both, and, in a vain attempt to bring them down, managed to damage the tower of Walmer Church and injure some of the men in the barracks there.'[26]

The Ministry strenuously denied this account of events, though even they were apparently not sure whether one of the aeroplanes sent up to engage the raiders even carried any armaments.

It was a further sign that aviation was in its infancy, as far as the general public was concerned, that the very appearance of an aircraft in the skies above Britain was considered newsworthy and attracted large crowds:

Army biplane over London

Considerable interest was aroused in North London shortly before eleven yesterday morning by the passage of a service biplane at a height of about 2,000 feet.[27]

Unfortunately, and despite official warnings to the contrary, the public showed the same fascination when the flying machines were of German origin:

The people . . . spent many hours in the streets and, lit with such light as the stars provided, calmly watched a spectacle designed to terrorise them . . . the streets became densely crowded, so eager was everyone to catch a sight of the Zeppelins.[28]

The correspondent went on to bemoan the uselessness of air-raid warnings:

We must all die, and, when dead, not one of us will be missed; but I suggest it is better to die unperturbed in comfortable beds than for our mangled remains to be collected from the roads.[29]

Or, as the *Southend Standard* rather more caustically put it:

We Britishers are not going to sit mum at home whenever there is a sight to be seen, out of mere consideration of safety.[30]

Ironically, on 12 August 1917 Southend would be the subject of another major air raid (after London had been ruled out as the Germans' target for the night, because of headwinds and fuel shortages). Many of the thirty-two people killed and forty-six injured in that raid were caught out in the street. But it seems likely this time that many of them were not in the streets as spectators, but because they had had no warning. No warning system had been in place in Southend at the time, and the public marched in protest to the Mayor's house about this afterwards. After another raid, when the public complained that no audible warning of the approach of the Germans had been given, the authorities explained that they did not fire warning maroons at night 'as they would unnecessarily disturb persons already under cover'.

Even if the authorities were assiduously to sound warnings, their efforts would hardly have been helped by newspaper reports that made air raids sound like an unmissable firework display:

As a moving, thrilling, tremendous demonstration, Monday night's raid was by far the most sensational 'show' we have experienced in London. The searchlights were whirling in great broad sword-blades of light; amid the flickers, our own questing aeroplanes darted like gnats, trailing lights hither and thither, and finally disappearing in the distant blue. Far away to the south-eastward, guns were rumbling and growling, the sound of them grew nearer and nearer . . . and then with a mighty roar the nearer batteries leapt into the attack . . . All the rest was one magnificent but frightening display of pyrotechnics.[31]

A letter from a Mrs Lindsay of Leigh-on-Sea rather confirmed the public's devil-may-care attitude to bombing:

What did you think of the Germans' visit to our part of the world? It was very exciting. They had a splendid fight in the air, which started at 2.10 and lasted a quarter of an hour. Then they made off Southend way but it was so foggy that we lost sight of them. It was thrilling to hear the boom of the big guns and the sharp firing from our aircraft, but no one seemed at all frightened.[32]

The newness of this form of warfare may account for the public's inability to appreciate its dangers fully, as this report shows:

Curious scenes were observed in the suburban shopping districts while the raid was in progress. Grocers, fruit and vegetable dealers and other tradesmen continued to serve customers who, between the ordering of one article and another, would go out into the street to observe progress. It was possible to hear such sentences as 'The shrapnel is bursting all around them now. And I shall want two pounds of butter, please'.[33]

Air raid precautions: the blackout

Even if the public were oblivious to the dangers of bombing, the authorities were alive to them. Within weeks of war breaking out, the first efforts were made – if not to blackout the metropolis, then at least to make it less easy for the Germans to navigate over:

The following notice has been issued by the Commissioner of Police for the Metropolis, and the assistance of the public generally is invited to give loyal effect to it:-

In order to render more difficult the identification of particular parts of London it is requested that arc lights, sky signs, illuminated fascias and powerful lights of all descriptions used outside for advertising, or brilliantly illuminating shop fronts be dispensed with.

Where the shop-front consists of a considerable area of glass, brilliantly lit from the inside a reduction of lighting intensity should be effected.

This request is made in connection with the observation of London lighting from above that will be made from a naval airship in the course of the next three or four days.[34]

The Admiralty sought similar measures in coastal areas. As some protection from the Zeppelins, a limited but more widespread and statutory blackout was introduced from October 1914. Illuminated signs were banned, shop-window displays dimmed and street lamps fitted with covers to stop their light shining upwards (though the pool of light they shone downwards onto the pavement might still have been a giveaway to any passing Zeppelin).

But much stricter regulations were introduced in December 1914. Because much street lighting was by gas, and had to be operated individually, they could not be switched off within the 5-minute warning the authorities expected to get of an air raid. Most of them had to be turned off permanently. The lights inside trams were dimmed to the minimum consistent with collecting the fares, street markets would enter a twilight world and car drivers would have to extinguish powerful headlights.

One paper had a blackout idea for the local authority, which it set out in the most florid and overblown language:

> *Now that the Egyptian darkness once more mantles the broad and narrow ways of the biscuit town the Corporation would find the ratepayers appreciating the system adopted in other towns, i.e. the whitening of the edges of the kerb at street crossings. It would prevent many a nasty jar and would result in the economising of adjectives.*[35]

This local authority thought it had the solution, which they advertised in the local paper:

NOTICE!

In order to assist in avoiding, as far as possible, the danger to life and property from

AIRCRAFT

THE COUNCIL, at a Special Meeting, have unanimously agreed that it is very desirable that

All shops

Should, for the present be

Closed at 6 p.m.

Except on Saturdays.

Considerable inconvenience to Foot Passengers will be saved if all persons using the Footpaths will

KEEP TO THE RIGHT[36]

But this would be of no help to Mrs Hannah Hill, who met her end at a road junction. The car that hit her was claimed to be doing little more than walking pace, but its headlamps were turned off, as were most of the street lamps. The driver was exonerated from all blame and a verdict of accidental death recorded. The Automobile Association warned of the danger of these new lighting regulations, especially to any pedestrians their members might run down, and the London Guarantee and Accident Company offered insurance cover for personal injuries sustained in the darkened street – a 5s a year premium could secure you compensation of £125, should you lose an eye or a limb; get yourself killed, and you could look forward to an even bigger payout. Further consequences of the blackout were early closing by retailers, who found too few shoppers willing to venture into the darkened streets, and the altering of the times of evening church services.

It seemed fairly clear that some citizens, at least, had not yet mastered the art of the blackout at home, as their local newspaper found it necessary to point out that:

> *It is not merely sufficient that measures should be taken to darken the front of the*

premises; equal care should be taken of the backs. There is a great deal to be remedied in this direction . . . There is ample evidence now to hand that during the recent raid where efficient measures were taken the town or district escaped and, on the other hand, where lights were incautiously shown, bombs were dropped in the vicinity with more or less destructive effect.[37]

Once again, the insurance industry rushed to the rescue of the citizen. Step forward the Gresham Insurance Company with its Union Jack policy, promising, for the outlay of as little as 17/4 (87p) a year, to pay the princely sum of £200 to anyone losing two eyes, two limbs (or one of each) or one life to a whole host of risks, including Zeppelin raids.

Air-raid warnings

There was a lull of some months between the main period of Zeppelin attacks on London and the Gotha bomber squadrons becoming fully operational. During this period, such air-raid precautions as had been put in place tended to lapse into disuse, and the renewal of bombing in 1917 was accompanied by calls for improved protection and warning. The authorities accordingly issued revised air-raid precautions instructions, though these did not appear to have been the fruit of mature consideration:

Protect yourself against Zeppelin attack with a Union Jack.

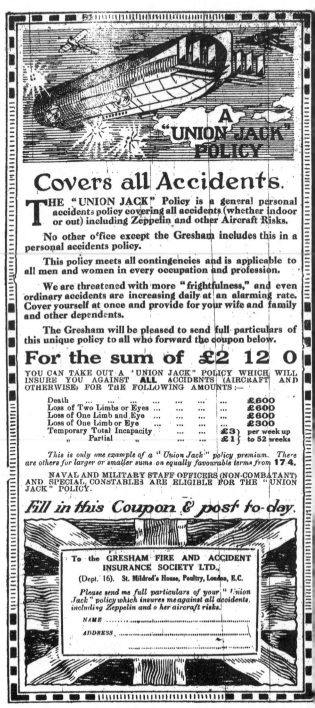

A "UNION JACK" POLICY

Covers all Accidents.

THE "UNION JACK" Policy is a general personal accidents policy covering all accidents (whether indoor or out) including Zeppelin and other Aircraft Risks.

No other office except the Gresham includes this in a personal accidents policy.

This policy meets all contingencies and is applicable to all men and women in every occupation and profession.

We are threatened with more "frightfulness," and even ordinary accidents are increasing daily at an alarming rate. Cover yourself at once and provide for your wife and family and other dependents.

The Gresham will be pleased to send full particulars of this unique policy to all who forward the coupon below.

For the sum of £2 12 0

YOU CAN TAKE OUT A 'UNION JACK" POLICY WHICH WILL INSURE YOU AGAINST **ALL** ACCIDENTS (AIRCRAFT AND OTHERWISE) FOR THE FOLLOWING AMOUNTS :—

Death		£600
Loss of Two Limbs or Eyes		£600
Loss of One Limb and Eye		£600
Loss of One Limb or Eye		£300
Temporary Total Incapacity	£3	per week up
„ Partial „	£1	to 52 weeks

This is only one example of a " Union Jack" policy premium. There are others for larger or smaller sums on equally favourable terms from **17.4.**

NAVAL AND MILITARY STAFF OFFICERS (NON-COMBATANT) AND SPECIAL CONSTABLES ARE ELIGIBLE FOR THE "UNION JACK" POLICY.

Fill in this Coupon & post to-day.

To the GRESHAM FIRE AND ACCIDENT INSURANCE SOCIETY LTD.,
(Dept. 16). St. Mildred's House, Poultry, London, E.C.

Please send me full particulars of your " Union Jack" policy which insures me against all accidents, including Zeppelin and o her aircraft risks.

NAME ....

ADDRESS ....

> *On hearing the sound signals or at night, the firing of anti-aircraft guns or*
> *explosion of bombs, persons in the open should at once take the most effective*
> *cover near at hand.*[38]

The Government was ambivalent about giving air-raid warnings, which some said simply had the effect of bringing a mass of the public out onto the streets to watch the spectacle. It was also claimed that they disrupted war production and damaged the morale of the civilian population. Nonetheless, it was eventually agreed to give all the population of London a 5-minute warning of a possible air raid. One of the advocates of a 5-minute warning was the MP for the City of London, Sir Frederick Banbury, who wanted the bells of St Paul's to be the warning signal in his constituency. His heart-warming reason for supporting the measure was that it would give the bank tellers in the financial district time to return all the cash to the safety of the vaults, before death and destruction started raining down on them.

But initially the only way the authorities could come up with to relay this warning to most of London was an arrangement whereby policemen, on foot or on bicycles, toured the streets wearing a placard saying 'POLICE NOTICE – TAKE COVER'. Once the danger had passed, they would retrace their steps with a placard saying 'ALL CLEAR'.

This was replaced in July 1917 by a centralised system based on County Hall and the capital's eighty fire stations. The public would be alerted by the firing of maroons. Even this did not work perfectly; on 22 July, a warning was received of a force of Gothas crossing the coast and this was relayed to County Hall. But it soon became clear that they were not targeting London and had indeed returned home. Unfortunately, no one thought to tell London this and, at 8.30 in the morning (15 minutes after the bombers had left British air space), most of the capital was sent scurrying for shelter. There they remained until somebody remembered them and the all clear was sounded at 10am.

But if London was not totally prepared for air raids, the Cheshire town of Macclesfield certainly was. Regardless of the fact that they were way outside the range of any of the German bombers of the day, the authorities advised residents:

> *Immediately the police receive notification of enemy aircraft approaching the*
> *town, the inhabitants will be warned by the firing of one ROCKET DISTRESS*
> *SIGNAL, such as is used as a distress signal on ships at sea and consist of a*
> *maroon which, when fired, gives a loud detonation at a height of 750 – 1000 feet.*

They added:

> *One hesitates in these times to say that anything is impossible, but an aeroplane*
> *raid on this district would appear to be an unlikely contingency.*[39]

Air-raid shelters

The provision of shelters was a vexed issue, particularly in London, the prime target for the bombers. At the height of the war, some 300,000 Londoners were taking nightly shelter in Underground stations, and a further 500,000 were sheltering in cellars and basements. The problem was especially acute in the densely occupied Docklands areas. Many Docklands houses did not have a cellar but even those that did were often so poorly built that they offered little protection. There were few parks and open spaces in which air-raid trenches could be dug and even some of the Underground stations serving that area tended to be on the surface, or too shallow to offer complete safety.

One person who ought to have known better about the dangers of air raids was one Police Constable Asquith. He found an unexploded bomb that had just gone through five floors of a pickle factory. He wrapped it in a sack, hoisted it up on his shoulder, carried it back to the police station and laid it on the charge-room table. It eventually had to be removed to the cells, because so many of his colleagues insisted on tinkering with it.

Evacuation: the alien invasion

The air raids in the autumn of 1917 onwards had one unexpected impact, which was felt well away from the areas actually bombed:

> *Reading, like other towns, has been hard-pressed to cope with the number of visitors from London. Friday last and the following days saw such an influx of people anxious to get out of the air raids that difficulty has been experienced in finding accommodation, but ultimately all were fixed up. Some have had to sleep in the waiting rooms at the railway stations until apartments were obtained, whilst others have even been accommodated at the police station. The visitors consist largely of Jews and at least 90 per cent are Russian Poles. In most cases they have been accompanied by a large number of children . . . The large increase in the town's population has meant a big run on the stocks of the local grocers and butchers.*[40]

Reading's Medical Officer of Health reported to the Council's Sanitary Committee on the scale of the problem:

> *There are, on the average, two thousand five hundred air raid refugees in Reading. Fifteen cases of overcrowding caused by them have come to my knowledge, and all but one of them have been abated. All the cases have been carefully enquired into and looked after; some refugee families have been induced to leave the town. I do not see that we can take further steps in the matter.*[41]

But this was not good enough for a group of businesses, based in the town and doing Government work. They petitioned the Home Office to make Reading a no-go area for aliens, under the Aliens Restriction (Consolidation) Order 1914. They drew the Home Secretary's attention to:

> *the serious and increasing hindrances which we are experiencing in the conduct of our business owing to the impossibility of obtaining dwelling houses for our employees.*
>
> *We have no doubt that the hindrances in question are caused, or very greatly aggravated, by the recent large and continuing influx of aliens or others who carry on no occupation in the Borough, but have come to Reading from the London area with a view to escape possible risk from air raids.*[42]

There were also complaints that these 'bombing dodgers', who had moved out of London to the region's provincial towns to escape the Zeppelins, were buying up properties and evicting long-standing local tenants from them. One particularly bitter letter came from one of the victims of these evictions:

> *Jews and Belgians are buying up properties by clubbing together and turning the permanent English residents out. Not content with eating the town out of food, they must needs turn us out. Very soon we shall be turned out of our country.*[43]

Some, particularly Londoners, thought that local people were being unnecessarily hostile to the newcomers and one, under the pen-name 'Cockney', issued this rebuke through the letters page:

> *London has from time immemorial been the Mecca of country folk seeking to make their position in life, and has opened its hospitable arms to those who have fled thence from political and religious persecution. During this war we have welcomed people from abroad and from our own coasts who were living in daily danger of their lives, irrespective of means or nationality, and it seems hard that Londoners who seek a similar haven in their own country should be shown so little sympathy.*[44]

A different kind of alien invasion was occurring in Kent. Traditionally, the poor of the East End of London migrated en masse each summer for a working holiday, picking hops. But most of them were now engaged in much better paid war work, or receiving separation allowances. Their places were taken by people higher up the social scale, not a few of whom were thought to be taking the opportunity to escape the threat of bombing for a few weeks.

Later developments

In July 1917, the first Zeppelin Giant bomber was supplied for use on the Western Front. These monsters were the size of a Second World War B29 Superfortress bomber (almost twice the size of a Gotha) and bigger than any British or German plane of the Second, never mind the First, World War. They had up to six engines and (with those engines supercharged) could reach an altitude of 19,000ft. However, they were not quite the ultimate terror weapon the Germans had in mind. Their huge weight and poor aerodynamics meant they could only manage 80mph, flying level in still air, and climbed only very slowly. They were cripplingly expensive and complicated to build, maintain and fly, especially for a Government that was running out of money – only sixteen were ever constructed. Their range was limited, as compromises had to be made between bomb load, fuel load and carrying the nine-man crew. For raids on England, they could not manage more than half their 2-ton maximum bomb load. They were, however, able to carry individual bombs of up to 1,000kg and it was one of these that flattened a large part of the Royal Hospital, Chelsea on 16 February 1918.

The first raid involving Giants – just two of them, supporting Gothas – took place in late September 1917. For all their sophistication they still could not pinpoint their target accurately. The raid scored no casualties and just £129 worth of damage to British agriculture. But possibly the most fearsome airborne weapon used by the Germans was a much smaller affair. Their previous incendiary bombs had been both unreliable and relatively ineffective when they did go off. But the new Elektron bomb, first used on

21 May 1918, was neither of these. It was largely made of magnesium alloys and burned ferociously. Hitherto, the British Fire Prevention Committee's advice to the public on incendiary bombs in 1918 was that:

> *fires caused by incendiary bombs may be prevented from spreading, regardless of the high temperatures generated at the actual seat of the outbreak, if water be promptly applied in fair bulk, force and continuity, say from a series of buckets energetically thrown or hand pumps vigorously worked.*

This advice would in fact make the fire from an Elektron bomb far worse. Late in the war, the Germans developed plans for large-scale raids, which would start huge fire-storms in London and Paris. In the event, the attacks, which were planned for 23 September, were called off just minutes before the aircraft took off. Manufacture of Elektron bombs ceased and existing supplies were returned to storage, as the German war effort went into a downward spiral leading to defeat. The design of the bombs used twenty-five years later to set fire to Dresden, Tokyo and other cities was almost identical to the Elektron.

Epilogue

By the end of the war, official attitudes towards the Royal Air Force (as it became in 1918) were very different to those prevailing at the start of the war. This editor acknowledged the change that had taken place in the understanding of the potential of aircraft to wage war:

> *Two years ago the particular and extremely disconcerting form of warfare which consists of machine gunning troops from low-flying aeroplanes was almost unheard of. Nowadays it has become an indispensable feature of British offensive operations. One of its chief objects is the demoralisation of the German infantry, and in this it is particularly successful.*[45]

That said, the aviators themselves did not always receive the same hero status accorded to their Battle of Britain counterparts in 1940:

> *I have often walked through the main streets and I have heard such leering remarks as 'Oh, a flyer; a turn in the trenches would do him good' and other insulting epithets.*[46]

Chapter 3
News From the Front Line

The weather has been awful, mud and water up to our middles, but the men are splendid, always 'merry and bright', never a murmur.

Letter home from Captain A. Bonham-Carter, published in the
Hampshire Chronicle
23 January 1915

Censorship

The local press had no shortage of first-hand accounts of life at the front in the First World War, and they ranged from the comical, through the mundane, to some truly harrowing accounts of bravery and suffering. The censors seemed to exercise a fairly light hand over anything in individual letters home that did not actually give away information of military value to the enemy, and few of the ordinary soldiers knew much of what was going on beyond their little part of the trenches. This is not to say that the censor never intervened. One serviceman's wife, receiving an envelope addressed in her husband's hand, expected to find a letter from him in it. Instead it contained a letter from the censor, saying 'Dear Mrs —, Your husband is quite well, but too communicative'.

If the censors gave individual soldiers a relatively free hand in writing home to their families about life in their piece of the trench, they were much more strict with what the newspapers might report about the broader conduct of the war. Not for the first time, nor the last, the press grumbled about the lack of news that they were allowed to relay to their readers. This from the earliest weeks of the war:

The papers are hard put to it to give their readers news from the theatre of war. The days of the

Soldiers can now make their own record of life in the front line.

special war correspondents are over. There is no room for a Russell or an Archibald Forbes.[1] We are not sure that the secrecy observed is not excessive. It is quite certain that, with the help of spies and aeroplanes, the German General Staff knows all that is worth knowing as to the disposition of the Allies, and the Allies are equally well-informed as to the positions occupied by the Germans. However, as secrecy is now insisted upon as an important element in the game of war, we are glad that we can play the game as well as our friends and enemies.[2]

As it happened, in that same edition the paper was actually given something to report, which they did, but not without irony:

At last it is permissible to state that the British Expeditionary Force has been safely landed on French soil. The movements of our continental service force have been known for some days to many people in this country. They have been described for a week in vivid detail in newspapers published on the continent. But Lord Kitchener desired the suppression of all such news in British newspapers, and he pays full tribute to the loyalty with which his wishes have been carried out.[3]

Certainly in Britain, the preparations for the departure of the BEF were shrouded in the tightest secrecy. Soldiers would be despatched without knowing their destination, and even their train crews would only be notified of it just before departure. Troop trains for the south coast ports would be despatched from the platform normally reserved for services to Windsor (itself a garrison town), so as to confuse any spies lurking at the station, and the captain of at least one troop ship was not told his destination until he was well out at sea. Ports were closed to the public, telegrams censored and any incoming newspapers that might be indiscreet were seized at the port of entry.

Many of the letters home from serving soldiers to friends and family found their way into the local newspapers. For the historian there is, however, a lack of surviving correspondence from Britain to the troops in the front line. This is thought to be largely due to the shortage of toilet paper in the trenches.

In the first weeks and months, the stalemate of the trenches had not yet been reached and it was still a war of movement. Unfortunately for the Allies, most of that movement was in retreat. A sergeant of the North Royal Lancashires described their journey (120 miles as the crow flies) from Mons in Belgium to Meaux, just 30 miles from Paris:

We had to march continuously for days and nights. If we were lucky, we had two hours' sleep out of twenty-four; if we were not lucky, we had to keep on the march. It was a common occurrence to see a whole company of men marching sound asleep. Our feet got so sore from the continual marching that many of us took off our boots, slung them over our shoulders and wrapped puttees around our feet.[4]

All friends at Christmas

Quite early in the war, the press reported events of which the Army hierarchy thoroughly disapproved, on the grounds that they might weaken the resolve of the troops to fight the enemy. Christmas 1914 saw extraordinary scenes of fraternisation between British and German troops on the Western Front, about which many soldiers wrote to their families. Their accounts started appearing in the papers early in 1915. Second Lieutenant Victor Johnson reported the exchanges of gunfire being turned into a fairground amusement:

> *The Germans fixed up targets for our men to shoot at just for fun and when we took a pot at the targets, the Germans would signal back with a shovel the result of the shot, whether it was a bull or a miss.*[5]

In parts of the line where there had been a terrific barrage on Christmas Eve, the guns fell silent throughout the Christmas holiday, leaving Gunner Richard Southern free to open his Christmas card from Princess Mary, and to eat his Christmas dinner of roast pork and vegetables, tinned Christmas pudding and half a pound of chocolate. In the evening, there was even a concert for them all to attend.

For some, the truce went further:

> *I shall never forget my Christmas Eve as long as I live. About six o'clock in the evening the Huns started showing torches in their trenches and we started shouting across to them 'A merry Christmas!' We then asked them if there was anyone sporting enough to come and have a chat and you will hardly believe it, but in a short time there were several came and met us half way, shook hands and smoked cigs with us. We afterwards sang carols to them and they sang their national songs to us. Our officers and theirs decided not to fire a shot until 10.30 that night. You cannot think how peaceful it was today.*[6]

> *Some of our people actually went into their trenches and stayed there for some time, being entertained by the enemy! All joined together in a sing-song, and it finally ended up with God save the King, in which the Saxons sang most heartily!*[7]

> *We were in the trenches for Christmas but came out on Boxing Day. They were the best three days we have spent. Not a shot was fired from 6 p.m. to the time we came away.*

> *Just fancy, the enemy came out of their holes shouting Christmas greetings on Christmas morning, and in five minutes dozens were meeting just half way, shaking hands in the best of style, exchanging cigarettes, tins of bully and even Christmas puddings. Did ever anyone hear of such a proceeding? They said 'Hang it all, Christmas is Christmas and we want our holiday'. . .*

> *They looked well and the four I shook hands with were men in their prime. I had one satisfaction and that was that they were evidently as cold and muddy as I was . . .*

The latter correspondent concluded his letter 'I am A1 except my feet and I can't tell whether it is frostbite or rheumatics.'[8]

Rifleman F. Maskill was even able to enlighten the Germans as to the progress of the war, during his brief Christmas fraternisation:

Some of our chaps played footer between the lines . . . I may tell you, it opened the eyes of the Germans when we told them about their defeats in Russia; also about their naval disasters. They had heard that their Army and Navy were everywhere victorious. Now they know, I wonder what it will lead to?[9]

Private Harold Platt only narrowly escaped frostbite:

We were over our knees in mud at Christmas and were so worn-out that we fell asleep and woke to find ourselves frozen to the ground. They had literally to dig us out, and to cut our boots off, and our feet were absolutely dead and black as coal . . . I have been lucky with my feet; some poor chaps have had to have their toes taken off; he just caught mine in time.[10]

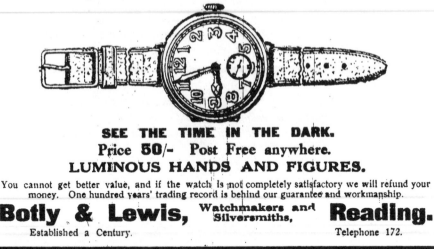
Despite experiences like Private Platt's, the *British Medical Journal* would later question many of the reported cases of frostbite, saying that they were simply rather advanced cases of chilblains. This did not stop shops back home doing a steady trade in frostbite preventative cream.

But the fraternisation was not always limited to that first Christmas. Some of the German troops (notably those from Saxony) were quite the opposite in outlook to their militaristic Prussian comrades, as this correspondent shows:

We have some of the Saxon corps opposite us; they seem to be extraordinarily good fellows. Yesterday some of the E—s had a long palaver with them. It resulted in one of our fellows meeting one of theirs . . . We groused about not being able to put a house in a state of defence, owing to their sniping, so it was eventually agreed upon to let us fix up the house if they could fix up the parapet.

However, during the fixing up of the house an officer [German] yelled out for our fellows to get down, as their Commanding Officer was coming along and he was afraid they should have to start plugging again. Before they started shooting he said that some of our fellows' heads weren't down, so he made gestures with his hand to keep down and when everybody was down he ordered a volley. He also apologised for the sniping at night, as we said it kept our men awake. He said only the 'Yonkers' [recruits] did it, to keep warm.[11]

In a French section of the trenches, French and German watering parties used to go to the river at the same time. By mutual agreement, both sides went unarmed, to avoid any possibility of fighting breaking out. Elsewhere, where an informal truce was in effect, it was agreed that:

If by any mischance, a single shot were fired it was not to be taken as an act of war and an apology would be accepted; also that firing would not be opened without due warning on both sides.[12]

Even where hostilities were taking place, it was still possible for the soldiers to feel pity for the men they were shooting. Private James Chalcroft, stationed at Mons:

At dawn next day we saw about twenty Germans scouting near our lines. Day was only just breaking; we could only just see them and we did not know how many more there were behind. They were coming across a field and when they were twenty yards away from us we got the order to fire. Poor beggars! There wasn't one of them got back to tell the tale. The firing gave our position away to the Germans, and they started shelling us for all they were worth. They were on a hill about three hundred yards away and that was where we lost a lot of our men.[13]

Hell in the trenches

Life in the trenches in winter could be hellish. This from a Mr H. Hine (rank unspecified):

We have had rather a hard time, standing in water over our knees for twelve hours. We were afraid to stand upright, as the bullets were whistling over our heads like rain . . . Then when we got out of the trenches our feet were little or no use; consequently over we went, continually slipping and sliding, until we arrived at the dugout – plastered in mud from head to foot . . . We made the best of Christmas in the circumstances – plenty of letters, parcels and grub.[14]

The water in Private W. Lowell's section of trench was even deeper, making the War Department's 'sparing' issue of rubber-topped boots look rather academic:

It is still raining and we have been up to our waists in water. The trenches are awful and, to make matters worse, the telephone would not work and I had to keep wading backwards and forwards, mending and laying new wires for three nights in succession. The place where I am has been very much bombed, especially a church. Even the tombstones and the coffins were dug up with the shells.[15]

Lieutenant Wells was wounded and taken prisoner during a German counter-attack, and described part of his 4¾-hour ordeal of shelling:

Eventually one of the last shells sent burst just behind us and down came the whole affair [the dug-out in which they were sheltering]. It was so close that for some time I did not know what had happened. Blood was dripping from my face on to my tunic and it was soon in an awful mess. I was pinned down and unable to move. The shelling had now stopped and only bombing and machine gun and rifle fire could be heard. Immediately afterwards, an officer from my own company came running past, shouting out 'hurry up and get back'. He saw I could not move and pulled off the debris. We set off together through the shell holes, mud up to our knees, etc., but we had not gone fifty yards before we were both hit, and dropped onto a small shell-hole, where we lay for six hours. The Germans were absolutely all around us, and had seen us lying there; we could do nothing but surrender.[16]

In the TRENCHES
or Training Camps your soldier's feet will be kept dry and comfortable if his boots are treated with

'Sportsman's Dubbing'

Makes boots waterproof under all conditions and the leather pliable. Send him a tin in his next parcel.
In tins 3d., 6d., 1/- & 2/-
or by post 6d., 10d., 1/4 and 2/8.
Manufacturers—
BRADLEY & BLISS, Ltd., 6 London St., Reading.
*Agent—*G. B. OSBORNE, 118 Broad St., Reading.

KEEPS YOUR FEET DRY

Even Sportsman's dubbing would struggle to cope with conditions in some of the trenches.

Sergeant Smart marvelled that he was even in a position to write to his family:

It is marvellous how some of us escape death. Only on Thursday I was in a fire trench and three men came in so I went out, as it was so small. I hadn't been out of the trench three minutes before a 'coal box' [a high-explosive shell] blew them to pieces. On Saturday I was standing up talking to a man of the guards when a shrapnel burst and killed him and wounded eight others. It was a wonder more weren't killed. I should like to tell you more, but I am not allowed to say very much . . . We have not got an officer left, they are all gone.[17]

Even if there was not shelling to contend with, just the day-to-day business of trying to make yourself comfortable in a muddy trench could be thoroughly dispiriting. This man describes his improvised tent:

A tarpaulin is drawn over the gap between [two wagons] and we have nestled down in the mud and straw as comfortably as possible. What with the rain splashes off the wheels, several weak spots in the tarpaulin, etc. we are kept

*fairly busy dodging the wet. I can count no less than seven buckets placed in
advantageous positions, not exactly to collect the 'nice soft water' for washing
but chiefly to prevent it running into our
'bedroom'. But, to be cheerful about it, the
'nice soft water' will save a long trek for
water for horses and men.[18]*

Corporal White of the 11th Rifle Brigade was
someone else who thought he detected a hint of
moisture in his trench:

*I am sorry I have not been able to write before
but have had rather a wet time. The last time
in the trenches was only forty-eight hours, but
it was quite enough. To start with the
communication trench was full of water, and
although we had boots up to the top of our
legs it was a lucky man that had not got his
boots full before we reached the fire trench.
When we got to our part of the trench there
was what was once a stream running from the
German lines right under our parapet, and the
continual rain had made the stream into a
river about fifty yards wide and still rising. To
further improve things the Germans pump the
water out of their trench and we get it. The fire
trench was flooded to a depth of about two
feet, and what dugouts were not fallen in were
flooded, so it was a case of wade, wade, wade
for forty-eight hours. The trench boards which
we had put down to walk on were either
floating about or stuck in the mud at the
bottom of the water to fall over. The first
morning the Germans gave us a good shelling,
just to keep us awake, and at night it was freezing cold, so you can guess we
were very glad when our time came to leave. Only about two men in the platoon
managed to keep on their feet the whole time. The rest, including myself, all fell
in, and it was nice and cold, especially having to let your clothes dry on you, but
we all came out cheerful and well. Now we are in a barn waiting for our next
turn and wondering if the tide will have gone out or if the Fleet will take over the
trench. We hope for one or the other. It's a fine life though, taking it all round.[19]*

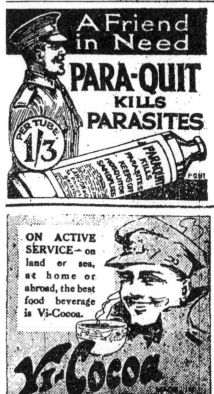

**Even insect pests are good business
for someone.**

Another correspondent at least had a roof on his accommodation, albeit little else in the
way of luxuries:

*We are just now living in a dugout some four feet high. The weather is bitterly
cold, and we have no stoves. We have tried the experiment of burning damp*

wood in a tin, bored with holes. Result, little warmth and a dense cloud of acrid smoke. The only ventilation is the 'door', a piece of sacking hung over the opening. After a short experience of the dense atmosphere, the fire is kicked out west, and we settle down to get what warmth is possible out of our blankets. We have not felt our feet for weeks but it doesn't do to complain of cold feet in war time. We still keep merry and bright, although we only have a candle to illuminate our underground dwelling, and it goes out every time a big gun is fired.[20]

But perhaps the most harrowing picture of life – and death – at the front is this account of some of the first poison gas victims:

When we got to the hospital we had no difficulty in finding out in which ward the men were as the noise of the poor devils trying to get breath was sufficient to direct us . . . There were about twenty of the worst cases in the ward on mattresses, all more or less in a sitting position propped up against the walls. Their faces, arms and hands were of a shiny grey-black colour, with mouths open and lead-glazed eyes, all swaying slightly backwards and forwards trying to get breath. It was the most appalling sight, all these poor black faces struggling, struggling for life . . . The effect of the gas is to fill the lungs with a watery, frothy matter which gradually increases and rises till it fills up the whole lungs and comes up to the mouth, then they die. It is suffocation, slow drowning, taking in some cases one or two days.[21]

Life and death

By 1915 pictures of men who had died on the Western Front were spread across the pages of many local newspapers. Coldstream Guardsman Gordon Mills was given a short spell of leave to come home and marry his long-term fiancée Madge Slowburn. He returned to France and within a week he was dead, and his new wife a widow. Equally touching was this letter home from Lance Corporal Charles Austen:

I am pleased to say that I am in the very best of health at present, excepting a very bad cold. We are up to our knees in water and mud in places, for we are having plenty of rain . . . But we all have hearts of iron, so we will stick it out for the sake of our King and Country . . . I am not downhearted and I don't want you to be, as I will do my duty with a good heart. So look forward to your loving son to come home when the time comes.[22]

But he would never come home, for a German shell killed him shortly afterwards.

Sergeant C. Bennett had the unusual distinction of being officially declared 'dead' twice and living to tell the tale. While serving with the Army in China he contracted enteric fever and was recorded as having bitten the dust, shortly before he actually recovered. He returned to the Army to serve on the Western Front, where he was wounded and sent home to recuperate. As he did so, he wondered why his Army pay was not coming through. It was only on his return to barracks that he learned that he was once again officially dead – his name was even on the regimental roll of honour. There was nothing his superior officer could do about it, so Bennett had to submit evidence from his employer, a clergyman and a police officer to the War Office to prove he was alive. The expression 'third time lucky' is not perhaps one to which he would have subscribed?

By contrast, Private Ernest Chinnery was prematurely diagnosed as 'well' by the Army. He reported in sick and had the charge of 'malingering – reporting sick without a cause' entered on his Army record by a sceptical doctor. Private Chinnery's response to this slur was to die, and the Coroner was called in to establish a cause of death. One thing he was able to rule out fairly quickly was malingering and the Coroner called for this to be removed from his record, finding him instead to be the victim of an advanced cancer.

Private Roland Mortimer had the unusual distinction of being both officially alive and dead in the same week – but not in the usual order. He was wounded in battle and, while having his wounds dressed, left his jacket behind. This was picked up by a comrade, who wore it into battle and was subsequently killed. When the body was recovered, the paybook and other contents of the jacket pockets led to the dead man being identified as Private Mortimer. The upshot was that his no-doubt distraught and bewildered family received, on consecutive days, a glowing obituary from his commanding officer, explaining that he had been shot through the heart, would have died instantly and would not have suffered, and a card from Mortimer himself, explaining that he had been wounded, but that it would only keep him out of action for a week or two.

The parents of Gunner William Towers had three months to mourn the death of their teenage son, after receiving confirmation of his death from the War Office. Then a prisoner-of-war swap was arranged with the Germans, exchanging prisoners no longer capable of active service. Among them was their son – alive but with a horrifying tale to tell. He and a group of comrades had been hit by a shell, which killed most of them and left William with terrible injuries. He had lost one leg, had sixteen shrapnel wounds in the other, as well as injuries to both arms, his chest and his face. One of his comrades had managed to drag him out of the line of fire before being forced to retreat, and the wounded man lay there in the rain for two days and nights before being found by the Germans and nursed back to (relative) health by them. His parents went to see him in hospital on his return and were delighted to report that he was 'in the best of spirits'.

The war nearly gave Able Seaman James Lennon the opportunity to attend his own funeral. He was posted as a deserter, then as one of the victims of a drowning incident, after a Petty Officer positively identified him as one of the deceased. He turned up at home just as the arrangements for his funeral were being finalised. His arrival put something of a dampener on the proceedings, which were duly cancelled.

Trench warfare can be fun

By contrast, some accounts of life in the trenches positively bubbled with enthusiasm. This new recruit waxed lyrical about his experience so far in the armed forces:

Who would be a civilian again?

It is half past three on a beautiful September afternoon and we have just been dismissed for the day. Stiff limbs loosened by the invigorating, though exacting exercise in the form of Swedish drill in the crisp morning air, followed by squad drill, give one a sense of physical wellbeing and a feeling that soldiering is, at

*any rate, an excellent change in many respects from the monotonous routine of
'driving the quill' and other avocations followed by those who have left their
situations in response to the call to arms.*[23]

And which idyllic section of the Western Front was this? Actually, an initial training
camp at Burnham Beeches in Buckinghamshire, an area delightfully free of German
activity.

At least Second Lieutenant Henry Birkby had actually reached the front. These are
extracts from his first two letters home:

*today I have been sniping the Huns from long range with telescopic sights. We
are in the support trenches, about 600 yards from Fritz's front line . . . I am
writing this in a dugout, which is simply lovely, in the centre of the earth, I
should think, and very comfortable. I am feeling simply great and can't
remember enjoying myself more than I did today.*

*To sum everything in a nutshell, I enjoyed my six days in the trenches immensely,
especially the last three in the front line. When anyone tells you there's no sport
in this war, don't you believe it.*[24]

Birkby was his battalion's sniping officer and, according to his Commanding Officer,
'showed great keenness and ability, being most fearless and at times almost reckless'. It
will therefore come as little surprise that his family received another letter on 20 April,
saying that he had died of his wounds.

Bizarrely, there were a few soldiers who positively revelled in artillery barrages, as a
way of enlivening dull sections of the front. Possibly out of consideration for those who
had had relatives killed in artillery barrages, the author of this letter home for once went
unidentified:

*We have had two artillery duels, which help to enliven us a bit. One gets so
horribly bored with the monotony of things here and a noisy artillery crowd is
very welcome, provided the enemy play fair and don't drop too close. We had a
few shells pretty close yesterday . . . For two or three months, if not longer, the
Germans have regularly searched all round with the shells, but there is not a
brick displaced here. It is really marvellous luck, and we are extremely grateful
to the German gunners. The village behind us has been badly knocked about
again and this time the village clock has been put out of action.*[25]

Trooper George Chapman was busy seeing off the Hun with bayonet charges, and
anticipated *Dad's Army*'s Corporal Jones by informing the readers that 'the Germans
don't like the steel'. Or, as one Highland trooper reportedly said of their successful
bayonet charge:

Man, ye should hae seen them rin miles frae the wee bit steel.[26]

Even being shot or blown up did not seem to curb some respondents' enthusiasm. One
of the participants at the Battle of Cambrai gave his family a remarkably upbeat account
of the experience, considering he was writing it from his hospital bed:

I was in the big push at Cambrai, and well we knew it. When I got hit we had to

lay out in 'no man's land' in a shell hole for ten hours. I crawled in when it was
dark. The fighting was very fierce, and we were subjected to very heavy firing.
The tanks did marvellous work; it was grand sport to be amongst so much fire.
We had a number of casualties, but I am glad to say that there were not many
killed. They were mostly wounded.[27]

This party of men had developed an entirely novel definition of fun:

The spirit of our boys was splendid. They simply loved the fun. One of them got
blown up by a shell. He seemed pretty dazed, but he picked himself up and came
along. All he said was 'Oh! There must be a war on after all, I suppose!'[28]

Sometimes the ingenuity of the troops could overcome conditions in the trenches. In one
section they constructed ovens from biscuit tins, and were able to boast to their people
at home of their five-course meal on Whit Monday:

Soup (Symingtons)

Fried steak and boiled potatoes

Tapioca (made with diluted condensed milk)

Bread, cheese and spring onions

Tea or coffee

If this were not luxury enough, they were allowed to go and have a bath, while their
uniforms were either baked or fumigated, to kill any bugs, and they were issued with a
complete new set of underwear (their old set would be washed and issued to some other
troops). They proudly boasted that 'no army ever went into battle so well equipped, nor
was so much thought devoted to their health and surroundings'. Second Lieutenant Victor
Johnson also got a bath, although his was in a vat in a disused brewery. One of his
officers, warned that the bath would smell of beer, complained that it was just his luck
that he could not smell it.

One trench catered for their occupants' artistic sensibilities with a piano that they had
'liberated' from what used to be a grand home nearby. It was played daily and stayed
perfectly in tune. The 6th Cheshires went one further and formed their own orchestra,
using harmonicas and instruments improvised out of bully beef tins to give their own
unique take on the popular songs of the day. This was to the tune of 'My little grey home
in the west':

I've a little wet home in a trench

Where the rainstorms continually drench

There's a dead cow close by

With her hooves towards the sky

And she gives off a beautiful stench.

Underneath in the place of a floor

There's a mass of wet mud and some straw

And the Jack Johnsons tear

This rain-sodden air

O'er my little wet home in the trench.[29]

On the subject of unofficial music, a Scottish regiment was visited by a delegation of foreign officers to watch one of their training exercises. Their guests were made to stand respectfully to attention while the regimental band played what the visitors were told was the Scottish national anthem. In fact it was the popular song of the day 'Beer, Beer, Glorious Beer'.

It could be possible to forget momentarily about the horrors of trench warfare, even when you were close to the front. This soldier found the so-far unspoilt landscape of Belgium near to his trench put him in mind of his native Surrey:

> *The weather has been glorious for the last few days, and yesterday morning I had a little walk around some fields in the sunshine. Some kiddies were playing around a farm and the birds singing cheerily; not a rifle or gun to be heard. The view was glorious. It made one forget for a few moments that there was a war on at all.*[30]

Corporal Graham Hodgson preferred his unspoiled view of licensed premises in 1914:

> *I am writing this in a village inn. I am feeling awfully well and am enjoying myself no end. All lights are out at eight o' clock, so we lie in our blankets and tell each other lies about the number of Germans we have shot, and the hairbreadth escapes we have had. Oh, it's a great life! . . . We will drink lager in Berlin before Christmas.*[31]

One volunteer who was certainly not going to allow trench warfare to cause his sartorial standards to slip was this former public schoolboy, who found himself (at least temporarily) in the trenches (a 'knut', you will recall, was one of those dedicated followers of Edwardian fashion):

> *A knut at the front*

> *The chauffeur of a General Staff motor car is completing his morning toilette in the open. After washing hands and face in a saucepan minus handle, which he has balanced on an empty petrol can, he carefully brushes his hair with an old nail brush, using the window of the car, in which he has just slept, as a looking glass. From the backward sweep he gives his rather long locks, and judging by his well-cut and clean, but dull brogue shoes it is clear that he has once been a 'knut', in spite of his oil-stained khaki service jacket and trousers.*[32]

Lest it should appear that the people in the trenches were having all the fun, submariner Charles Allen wrote home to his family:

> *I am having the time of my life. As time is getting short now we expect to be leaving about — out for some more sport. We had a good 'bag' last time, nine ships including one battleship, eight gunboats and about twenty sailing ships, beside troop ships, and blew up a bridge. Take it all round we had a good time.*[33]

First-hand accounts of the war in the air are inevitably much less common than those from the trenches, but this aviator shared his experience with his local paper:

> *Captain H.K. and I were leaders of the expedition. We were escort to the*

*reconnaissance and had one other to help us, three machines all told. We left at
3.45 a.m. and proceeded to climb. We found all three machines were different in
speed, ours fastest, then the reconnaissance, then the other. The rec. went up to
10,000 feet and we could only get to 9000. We crossed the lines in the most
terrific hail of 'archies' [anti-aircraft guns] I have ever had. Our machine was
hit twice and the other escort had 36 holes in him, while the rec. was untouched.
Soon as we got over the lines I saw friend Immelman (a well-known enemy
airman) in a very fast 'Fokker Scout' coming up behind the top machine which
was over our heads. We had all agreed to be ready for him, but the observer in
the rec. did not see him. We couldn't do anything to help him but blazed at
Immelman to try to attract our man's attention. Of course he didn't hear us. Then
we saw Immelman open his engine and dive straight on to their tail. It was the
most horrible moment, knowing he is a dead shot, and not being able to help.
They saw him just before it was too late, and dodged. He got a lot of bullets into
their machine, but none serious.*

*Our chap then got out his machine gun and gave him a couple of sharp bursts.
He then went off and hung around, going for us alternately but never coming
near again. (He was only 120 yards from the rec. when they saw him, and comes
nearer than that to fire.) If only the brute had attacked us instead of the other, he
would have been 'for it', as I had a trick up my sleeve to catch him with, and
would have let him have a full drum of ammunition. I simply couldn't have
missed him, but it was just a bit of bad luck that he should have gone for the
wrong machine. We then went on quite peacefully, and beat off three more Huns
on the way back.*[34]

Horror and heroism

The papers were full of the heroic deeds of our boys. Trooper Arthur Andrews, serving
in the Dardanelles, found himself badly wounded in no-man's-land, next to a man who
was literally on fire:

*I should not have moved at all only that one of our fellows was lying about five
yards from me, all in flames; he was being burnt to death and nothing whatever
could save him. The flames threw up a brilliant light, and of course made me an
excellent target. Bullets were whizzing all around me, but fortunately I escaped
being hit.*[35]

It took Andrews an hour to drag himself the 30yd to another shell hole where a comrade,
Frederick Potts, was taking shelter. Here is Potts' own account of the action:

*On going into action, we had to run across an open space to the foot of some
hills, a distance, I should think, of one-and-a-half miles, while the enemy were
pelting shrapnel into us. Just a wee bit hot. The Berkshires did not lose many
men in this venture, though some regiments suffered very severely. The next move
was an advance up the hill; it was perfect hell, chaps being mown down anyhow.
When about a quarter of a mile from the summit we were told to get ready to
charge. Not a man faltered. We had already captured a Turkish trench, and when*

the order was given to charge, over we went. About twenty yards the other side I received a wound in the thigh; it completely knocked me off my feet, and I had to lie there. Presently another of our chaps crawled to where I was; he was shot in the groin.

We stayed where we were all that night, suffering very much from thirst, but it was much worse the next day. It seemed as if we should go mad for the want of a drink. When night came, we decided to move, if possible. This was no light job, as firing had been going on all around us. One bullet actually grazed my ear, but we managed it somehow. Then we were able to get some water off a man who had been killed. Rather a painful job taking it, but one of necessity. We found a hiding place for the remainder of the night, and the next day we dare not show ourselves, for fear of snipers. Oh! the thirst. I crawled from one body to another, getting water. When we got any it was like wine, although it was nearly boiling. When night came we decided that anything was better than to die of thirst, so we crawled to where we thought we should find some English lines.

The other chap could hardly move, and after a few yards had to give up. So I found a shovel and he lay on it and I dragged him down the hill bit by bit for about three-quarters of a mile. Before we started, I prayed as I have never prayed before for strength, help and guidance and felt confident we should win, though when the bottom of the hill was reached we came to a wood. I left the other chap to find a way through. I had not gone more than twenty yards when I received the command to 'halt'. I had by luck struck a British trench, where we were treated with every kindness . . . From here we were carried to a Field Ambulance Dressing Station and had our wounds dressed.[36]

Potts was awarded the VC for his gallantry and, many years later, Andrews would be one of the mourners at his funeral.

The bestial Hun

Every week, the paper carried reports of the bestiality and deceit practised by the enemy. No cruelty or underhand treatment appeared to be beneath them (though we might wonder today how much of it was the product of Allied propagandists' fertile imaginations). It was said they lured unsuspecting Allied troops into the line of fire by pretending to be French or to surrender, used local people as human shields, deliberately shelled buildings clearly marked as Red Cross hospitals or, having captured said hospitals, bayoneted the patients in their beds. One Allied civilian was treated by a British Army medic, after a German soldier cut her finger off to steal her wedding ring. The Germans were even brutal towards their own. One Allied soldier reported seeing them throwing badly wounded German troops into a mass grave with dead comrades. The Allies rescued these wounded Germans, who freely admitted (some would say with commendable understatement) to being 'fed up' with the entire business.

By 1915, the Allies were more wise to German deception. As one Irish guard reported, they:

had orders to take no notice of anyone coming and saying they were English, as

about a hundred Germans advanced onto the Irish Guards, saying they were
Coldstream Guards; but the Irish Guards were 'not having any', for when the
Germans reached about fifty yards of our trenches we opened fire upon them,
and only one out of the lot was left alive.[37]

Corporal Frederick Toovey told the newspaper of his experience of being captured by the Hun. He and his colleagues were told to reveal details of their troop positions and, when they refused, they were told they would be tortured and killed. They actually saw French and Belgian soldiers who had similarly refused having their ears cut off, their eyes gouged out and other unspeakable acts performed on them, prior to their execution. Toovey and his colleagues had been rescued by an Allied advance in the nick of time. Lance Corporal Herbert Lewin was also captured by the Germans, and his thrilling account of his escape from his prisoner-of-war camp was serialised by his local paper.

It was not just serving soldiers that allegedly fell victim to the Germans' war crimes. A report in the *Henley Standard* brought to light accounts of civilian atrocities. After a German officer was shot by a civilian in Aerschot, it was claimed that women and children were killed in reprisal. The Germans claimed they had died by unwisely venturing out of their houses in the middle of a fire-fight between the two armies, but this could not explain why their hands and feet had been cut off. The same report also carried an account of an old man, who had apparently been hung by his arms from the rafters of his house and roasted to death over a bonfire. In Villerupt, the village church was burned, with the villagers inside, after the church tower was allegedly used as an observation post. A single shot, fired from another village, led to the entire street from which it was fired being razed to the ground and its inhabitants executed. From all over Belgium, there were reports of civilians being more or less randomly slaughtered.

No war crime was too petty for the enemy to engage in. German forces occupying a town near Liège apparently insisted that all civilians should show their respect to officers by removing their hats and saluting when they passed by:

Anyone failing in this must expect a German soldier to exact respect from him by
any method.[38]

For their part, retreating Austrian soldiers were said to have left behind cigarettes laced with an explosive charge and some other Germans poisoned abandoned animal feed with strychnine. For some, almost worse than any of this was the desecration of France's historic heritage. This was one man's reaction to the sacking and burning of Rheims Cathedral:

Grim remembrance of this abominable deed will always remain with me as with
all who saw it. The sight of the flames devouring this splendid relic of the
thirteenth century, which took 150 years to build, and which has been respected
through all the countless wars that have been waged in France since then, was
terrible and yet fascinating. It was as though we were watching something
supernatural – the work of the fiends themselves. [39]

The Germans also told each other atrocity stories about the British. Captured German sailors told their captors that they had been warned that, if taken prisoner, they would be tied to the muzzles of British guns and blown to pieces. This led to some German sailors jumping overboard and some thirty of them allegedly cutting their own throats, rather than face capture. Another group of terrified German captives had apparently been persuaded by their officers that the Allies were all cannibals, and ate their prisoners of war.

The reports of atrocities in the papers had one unintended consequence. An Oxfordshire primary school teacher set his pupils to write a composition on the subject of the war, and what came back from them was a lot of very frightened anticipation of German atrocities, should they ever invade. One youngster wrote:

> *I think that the Germans are in our country and that they will kill us, or eat us, or drown us. My mother said that if the Germans do come over here she will drown us before they do come over. The Kaiser has got new-monnyer [sic] and will soon die, and I said that it serves him right.[40]*

Even as the Germans made their final retreat in late 1918, their demonisation continued, as this editorial calling for extreme reprisals shows:

> *In his forced retreat the German is showing once more the mark of the beast, burning and destroying all that he is forced to relinquish.*
>
> *This is done with a calculated purpose; it is to weaken France permanently, and to make her an easier prey in the 'next war', which Prussia, if allowed to survive as a powerful state, will begin planning before the ink on the peace treaty is dry.*
>
> *If nothing is done, the whole of the occupied region will be left a desert. But if the German people are made to understand that they will pay in kind for every fraction of damage done, and that a town across the Rhine will be razed to the ground for every town sacked and devastated by the Germans, fear may prompt what decency and humanity are powerless to dictate . . .*
>
> *The German peoples have an idea that they have only to cry 'Kamerad' at the last and all will be forgiven. They have no conception of the feeling against their race, or of the stern resolve which possesses nine people out of ten in this country, in France and in America. They are in for a rude awakening.[41]*

Always look on the bright side . . .

As in any war, rumour and counter-rumour abounded, and the Government was keen to put a stop to it. Within weeks of the outbreak of hostilities, the government's Press Bureau issued this statement:

> *The public are warned against placing the slightest reliance on the many rumours that are current regarding alleged victories or defeats and the arrival of wounded men or disabled ships in this country. These are, without exception, baseless. The public may be confident that any news of successes or reverses to the British arms will be communicated officially without delay.[42]*

But how much reliance could be placed on the official communiqués? To look at the early war reports in the local papers, it would seem that on all fronts the enemy were being driven back with huge losses, their navies sunk and their air forces shot down in flames. This made it all the more difficult to understand how, in separate reports, the Germans appeared to be making steady progress into Belgium and northern France. Even so, it was a concern to the Allied leadership that the message of our triumphs was not being taken at face value by everybody. A leading article in *The Times*, taken up locally, complained that:

> *all sorts of absurd and unfounded rumours have been circulated by light-headed and irresponsible individuals. There have been dire reports of mishaps suffered by the Allies, of German victories, of insurrection in the French capital and even of heavy British casualties by land and sea.*

> *Men and women of ordinary common sense need hardly be assured that these legends are false. It is not the practice of British Governments to suppress or minimise 'regrettable incidents' or even disasters when they befall us . . . We have not the slightest doubt that the War Office will in future take the public into its confidence as readily as the Admiralty, and as readily as they did throughout the Boer War, and that relatives and friends of our sailors and soldiers will receive at the earliest moment all information of any casualties incurred, so far as the interests of the services allow.[43]*

One indicator of the accuracy of official reports might be taken from the following extracts:

> *Great battle on the Somme*

> *A good day for the allies*

> *Heavy enemy losses[44]*

> *About half past seven this morning a vigorous attack was launched by the British Army . . . It is too early yet to give anything but the barest particulars, as the fighting is developing in intensity, but the British troops have already occupied the German front line . . . As far as can be ascertained our casualties have not been heavy.[45]*

> *The offensive at last!*

> *Probably the greatest event in the war, and it may be the most momentous event in European history, will be dated from July 1. After nearly two years of intense struggle, marked by episodes of unprecedented violence; after the revelation of the resources and capacity of the enemy which was staggering to the imagination; after the painful experience of losses on a large scale and of the necessity of standing on defence against the most unscrupulous and pitiless of aggressors – the Allies have been able to start what is technically known as 'the Great Offensive'. It has started auspiciously. If we were in a buoyant mood and*

easily exhilarated, we might almost justify, on the first reports, a great ebullition of satisfaction and indulge in forecasts of stupendous success. But this is not only unreasonable, but would carry with it an element of danger. For the progress we made we may be thankful. It is full of hope and assurance of good things to follow. We may anticipate that a far-reaching plan has been well thought out by master minds. There is every reason to believe that the military leaders have accumulated men and metal which will enable them to overcome the opposition of the enemy and eventually to push him back stage by stage. But to presume the end is even in sight savours of grotesqueness in these days of stupendous operation.[46]

The event they were 'describing' was the first day of the Battle of the Somme, now seen as the most disastrous day in the entire history of the British Army. On the morning of 1 July 1916, almost 750,000 Allied troops, most of them British, launched an offensive on the part of the Western Front between Amiens and Peronne. By the end of the day, the Expeditionary Force had suffered almost 60,000 casualties. Nonetheless, over the days and weeks that followed, the newspaper reports claimed a virtually unbroken string of successes, until the casual reader might be forgiven for thinking that the Allies were camped outside the gates of Berlin. In reality, the campaign dragged on until November, leaving the British with 420,000 casualties and little or no territorial gain to show for it.

In similar vein, the newspapers also scored the naval battle at Jutland, today seen as one where the Germans arguably came off rather better, as a decisive Allied victory:

Was the Battle of Jutland a great naval victory for the British? Were the arrangements and results satisfactory? Was our superiority demonstrated? These are the questions that have been in men's minds. They are answered in the long-awaited despatch from Sir John Jellicoe. It is couched in restrained language, but describes a naval action on a scale unprecedented in history . . . This was a decisive victory. Except for the gallant lives that have been lost we can look back with thankfulness as well as pride upon this, the greatest naval battle in the history of the world. The enemy losses were not only proportionately but absolutely much heavier than our own.[47]

The Tommies (or at least those who put words of propaganda into their mouths) could apparently see the bright side of everything. One even claimed that a good thing about Flanders mud was that it kept you warm:

I never had a cold until I got here and cleaned the mud off.[48]

Chapter 4

Volunteers, Conscripts and Objectors

Compulsory service is, I believe, as distasteful to the nation as it is incompatible with the conditions of an army like ours, which has such a large proportion of its units on foreign service. I hold, moreover, that the man who voluntarily serves is more to be relied upon as a good fighting soldier than is he who is compelled to bear arms.

Lord Roberts – Former Commander of the British Armed Forces

Conscription is now the law in this country of free tradition. Our hard-won liberties have been violated. Conscription means the desecration of principles that we have long held dear; it involves the subordination of civil liberties to military dictation; it imperils the freedom of individual conscience and establishes in our midst that militarism which menaces all social graces and divides the people of all nations.

From a No-Conscription Fellowship leaflet

Have you a butler, groom, chauffeur, gardener or gamekeeper serving you who at this moment should be serving his king and country?'

Recruitment poster © 1915

The call for volunteers

Unlike most Continental countries, Britain in 1914 had no tradition of conscription. At the outbreak of war, the British Army numbered just 247,432 regular troops. About 120,000 of these were despatched to the Continent in the British Expeditionary Force – what the Kaiser allegedly referred to as Britain's 'contemptible little army'. This epithet was on account of its size, which was rather less than the number of troops 'brave little Belgium' could muster, rather than its fighting abilities. For its part, Germany had an army of some 34 divisions (or 700,000 men) just at the northern tip of its drive into France, and expected to sweep all opposition before it. It was clear from the outset that Britain would need many more troops.

Within days of the outbreak of war, Kitchener began a campaign to attract volunteers.

His initial recruitment drive sought a hundred-thousand men for the armed forces. They were looking for able-bodied men aged 19 to 30 (single or married) or ex-servicemen up to the age of 42. They were to sign up for three years, or the duration of the war (few then could believe that it would last as long as three years). This campaign had the whole-hearted editorial support of the local press:

> *For fifty years the military chiefs in Prussia have been pursuing with deadly resolution a relentless policy of crushing the neighbouring nations one by one, in the hope that by devastating other lands and ruining their commerce, Prussia would eventually dominate the world . . .*

His and hers recruitment propaganda, showing the important role of women in getting men to sign up.

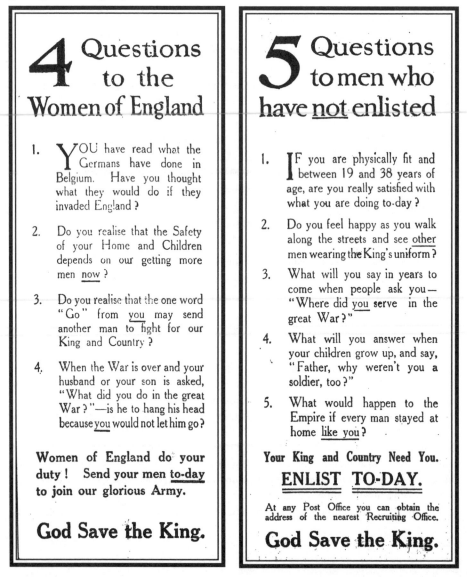

4 Questions to the Women of England

1. YOU have read what the Germans have done in Belgium. Have you thought what they would do if they invaded England?

2. Do you realise that the Safety of your Home and Children depends on our getting more men now?

3. Do you realise that the one word "Go" from you may send another man to fight for our King and Country?

4. When the War is over and your husband or your son is asked, "What did you do in the great War?"—is he to hang his head because you would not let him go?

Women of England do your duty! Send your men to-day to join our glorious Army.

God Save the King.

5 Questions to men who have not enlisted

1. IF you are physically fit and between 19 and 38 years of age, are you really satisfied with what you are doing to-day?

2. Do you feel happy as you walk along the streets and see other men wearing the King's uniform?

3. What will you say in years to come when people ask you— "Where did you serve in the great War?"

4. What will you answer when your children grow up, and say, "Father, why weren't you a soldier, too?"

5. What would happen to the Empire if every man stayed at home like you?

Your King and Country Need You.

ENLIST TO-DAY.

At any Post Office you can obtain the address of the nearest Recruiting Office.

God Save the King.

Young men of Reading. Are you content . . . to see your homes destroyed, your families slaughtered in cold blood and your liberties abolished under the iron heel of this brutal military tyranny? If not, the only remedy lies in your hands. Join Lord Kitchener's Army.[1]

The appeal initially got some 33,000 volunteers a day. Within 3 weeks, the age limit was raised to 35, and by mid-September Kitchener already had over 500,000 volunteers. But even this would not be enough to feed the killing fields of Flanders and France indefinitely. Not only the age but also the physical requirements of the volunteers were progressively relaxed. At first, recruits needed to be 5ft 6in tall, with a 35in chest. By May of 1915, 5ft 3in would suffice, and the age limit was further raised to 40 years; and in July 'bantam battalions' of men between 5ft and 5ft 3in began to be formed. The recruitment effort would later also relax fitness criteria:

A Soldier of the KING.

AFTER the War every man who has served will command his Country's gratitude. He will be looked up to and *respected* because he answered his country's call.

The Regiments at the Front are covering themselves with Glory.

Field-Marshal Sir John French wrote in an Order of the day,

"It is an Honour to belong to such an Army."

Every fit man from 19 to 38 is eligible for this great honour. Friends can join in a body, and serve together in the same regiment.

Rapid Promotion.

There is rapid promotion for intelligence and zeal. Hundreds who enlisted as private soldiers have already become officers because of their merits and courage, and thousands have reached non-commissioned rank.

Enlist To-day.

At any Post Office you can obtain the address of the nearest Recruiting Office. **Enter your name to-day on the Nation's Roll of Honour and do your part.**

GOD SAVE THE KING.

In a circular note issued from the War Office it is stated that . . . a very large percentage of the recruits will undoubtedly be drawn from a class whose civil occupations are of a sedentary character. This must be borne in mind, and physical training of such recruits will be modified accordingly in order to accustom them gradually to physical exercises.[2]

One of the more novel proposals for recruitment came from a James Mellor, who suggested allowing convicted prisoners to sign up for the armed forces and 'show that they are made of better metal than they are generally given credit for'. Another reason for getting yourself into uniform was to make yourself irresistible to women and the object of universal male admiration:

Tommy Atkins has been the man of the moment in Reading this week and the breast of many a youthful Territorial must have swelled with pride at the cheers which the uniform he wears have occasioned. In the past, the passing of a company of our citizen soldiers would have aroused little interest and no enthusiasm. The references of the unthoughtful may sometimes have been far from complimentary, but when Britain's last efforts to secure peace failed and war was officially declared between this country and Germany, the Territorials, as a force for home defence, assumed a new importance and many a young civilian has been heard to express a regret that he has never joined their ranks.[3]

This paper went into patriotic overdrive as a group of reservists reported for duty:

alert, well-built men, they commanded the admiration of those who assembled outside the barrack gates to witness their arrival. Here was a burly navvy; here, a weather-beaten son of the soil, straight from the harvest field; and there, the no less healthy and alert artisan . . . some of them bought what was required wrapped in handkerchiefs. What struck the observer was the note of quiet determination on the faces of the men as they jauntily swung into the barracks. Some of the lively spirits rolled up singing such popular airs as 'Fall in and follow me' and 'I don't care what becomes of me'.[4]

Ironically, it seemed that retreat had a more positive effect upon recruitment than advances, for, despite the bad news in the first months of war, men were coming forward to sign up in considerable numbers. In many cases, they were actively encouraged to do so by their employers, many of whom promised to keep the posts of volunteers open for them to return to, after the war, and to take care of their dependents in the meantime. For their part, some would not only give their staff leave of absence to go and fight, they would make up their Army pay to what it would have been, had they remained in their employ.

The Army appeared to be overwhelmed by the sudden influx of volunteers when war broke out. One barracks, which was designed to accommodate about 300 men, found itself with 2,000 residents, and only 4 officers left to organise them. A spokesman said: 'we are not surprised that there was some little disarrangement and confusion', these little disarrangements apparently including some of the men having nothing to eat and having to sleep in the open air. A partial solution was found by the local Wesleyan Hall opening its doors to them, to provide cheap food and shelter (through a public appeal for cash, blankets and foodstuffs). Other would-be recruits were sent home on a retainer of 3*s* (15p) a day, to wait for recall as soon as the Army could cope with them.

Pressures to volunteer

Britain may have had a voluntary army in the first half of the war, but the pressure on men to volunteer was considerable. Women took on a major role in driving men into uniform, and the authorities played on this. One Army recruitment poster read:

To the young women of London

*Is your 'best boy' wearing khaki? If not, don't **you think** he should be?*

*If he does not think that you and your country are worth fighting for – do you think he is **worthy** of you?*

Don't pity the girl who is alone – her young man is probably a soldier – fighting for her and her country – and for YOU.

*If your young man neglects his duty to his King and Country, the time may come when he will **neglect you**.*

*Think it over – and then ask him to **Join the Army today***

The Order of the White Feather was initiated by Admiral Charles Fitzgerald in August 1914. The aim was simple – to shame people into volunteering by the participant – usually a young woman – presenting anyone seen in the street who looked vaguely of recruitable age and was not in uniform with a white feather, as a symbol of their cowardice. Kitchener gave a speech in which he sanctioned this kind of moral blackmail:

> *The women could play a great part in the emergency by using their influence
> with their husbands and sons to take their proper share in their country's
> defence, and every girl who had a sweetheart should tell him that she would not
> walk out with him again until he had done his part in licking the Germans.*[5]

There were, of course, many reasons why men would not be in uniform. They could have failed the medical, be engaged in civilian work of national importance, or they could be serving men on leave, or invalided out – at least one recipient of a white feather was the holder of a VC. Some women used it to get rid of unwanted boyfriends. One such advertisement in the personal column of *The Times* read:

> *Jack F.G. If you are not in khaki by the 20th I shall cut you dead. Ethel M.*[6]

It became enough of a problem to prompt the Government to issue the Silver War Badge, showing that the wearer was contributing to the war effort. Some of the railway companies issued their staff with similar badges, to show that they were not shirkers, but engaged on work of national importance. When the women started buttonholing state employees, the Home Secretary was asked to have them arrested, and when Lord Derby's recruitment campaign introduced a form of deferred call-up for volunteers, the recruits were issued with blue armbands with a red crown, to show their standing as volunteers.

White feathers through the letterbox may also have been a problem for, in August 1915, it was announced that the local recruiting office was supplying enlisted men with patriotic badges to be displayed in the window of their family home, saying 'A man from this house is serving his King and country'.

In similar vein to the Order of the White Feather, Baroness Orczy founded the Active Service League, whose members swore the following oath:

> *At this hour of England's greatest peril and desperate need, I do hereby pledge
> myself most solemnly in the name of my King and Country to persuade every
> man I know to offer his services to the country, and I also pledge myself never to
> be seen in public with any man who, being in every way fit and free for service,
> has refused to respond to his country's call.*

The Conservative ladies of Newbury gathered to discuss how they could best encourage men to volunteer. Lady Caernavon told the meeting of an inspiring encounter she had had at Notley Hospital:

> *There was one poor fellow with a shattered arm, but he was not complaining. He*

said to the doctor 'Please sir, get me well as quickly as you can, so that I can
have another smack at them'. What a splendid spirit! What inspiring bravery![7]

One of the more (to us) implausible leading lights of the recruitment campaign was Horatio Bottomley (1860–1933) – financier, journalist, newspaper proprietor, populist politician, Member of Parliament, but mostly remembered today as a notorious swindler. He founded the jingoistic journal *John Bull* in 1906 and served as a Member of Parliament from 1908 until 1912, when bankruptcy forced him to resign his seat. When war broke out, *John Bull* became even more ferociously patriotic, calling for Germany to be 'wiped off the face of Europe', its colonies and navy confiscated and German nationals living in Britain made to wear a distinctive badge (like the Jews in Nazi Germany).

Bottomley was a gifted mob orator, who took to organising a series of what were variously recruitment meetings, patriotic war lectures, promotions of *John Bull* and near music-hall turns that drew huge audiences. One at the Royal Opera House allegedly drew an audience of 20,000 (only 5,000 of whom could gain admittance). At another meeting in Hull, Bottomley claimed to have recruited a thousand men in a single evening.

Bottomley naturally charged for his services. His fees ranged from £25 for a straightforward recruitment meeting to whatever he could get (for one engagement £1,000) for dispensing general patriotism. Much of this money was laundered through his War Charity Fund (which, in reality, never received a penny of it). He also charged *John Bull* a total of £22,000 for his promotional efforts on its behalf and launched a fraudulent Victory Bond scheme, which earned him £900,000. He would later be sentenced to seven years' prison for fraud and died in alcoholic poverty.

The Derby Scheme

But even with white feathers and Kitchener's relaxation of the standards needed to join up, a policy based on voluntary recruits was bound eventually to run out of steam. Conscription was not something the Asquith Government felt comfortable with, and they cast about for an alternative. Lord Derby, a leading anti-conscriptionist, was appointed Director of Recruitment in October 1915. His scheme was based upon a register, compiled the previous July. Many, including the parliamentary opposition, were afraid that this national register was the thin end of a compulsory conscription wedge, but Asquith was at pains to reassure them that this was not the case, as was the editor of this newspaper:

There is nothing whatsoever in the Bill to frighten the most timorous of anti-
conscriptionists; the system is founded on pure voluntaryism [sic]; the only
compulsory part in it is that you must register.[8]

The scheme called upon (but did not require) all men on the register aged 18 to 41 to 'attest' – that is, to agree to serve at some time in the future, as and when required. Derby received a rapturous response as he toured the country, seeking recruits. In St Helens he packed out both the town's theatre and an overflow meeting in the Town Hall, and still left some 8,000 would-be attendees in the street outside. Some 2½ million signed up and

EVERY PICTURE TELLS A STORY.

Men were confronted on every side with pressure to sign up.

were placed in one of 46 groups, according to age and marital status, with single men aged 18 being the first group to be called up and 41-year-old married men the last.

However, a large part of the 2½ million were declared exempt from military service, being either munitions workers, employees in key Government departments or in a host of 'certified occupations' considered essential to the war effort. In total, the Derby Scheme provided less than 350,000 additional troops, and was abandoned in December 1915.

Conscription

But the move to compulsion for human recruits was still not one that the authorities found it easy to make. This editorial rehearsed some of the philosophical arguments for voluntarism:

> *With all its drawbacks, the voluntary system has done so much for the country that we may all hope that it will see us through the war. It calls out a high resolve of self-consecration, it creates an army superior, we firmly believe, to any other. It raises the national character and makes war a matter of conscience, rather*

than of habit and professional obedience. Hence it makes for peace, not for militarism.[9]

But as the demand for additional men at the front increased and the supply of willing volunteers began to be exhausted, so the pressure to introduce conscription increased. This was bitterly opposed by groups like the No-Conscription Fellowship. The Fellowship was founded by two pacifists, Clifford Allen and Fenner Brockway. It was a pacifist organisation, rather than just one opposed to compulsory conscription (as opposed to voluntary recruitment). Both founders served time in prison for their cause, having been arrested for distributing anti-conscription leaflets and then refusing to pay the fines imposed by the court. Another of its leading lights, C.H. Allen, was also arrested, confined to a straitjacket and forcibly fed through the nose with a tube, before serving a year's hard labour.

The Derby branch of the Fellowship was infiltrated by MI5 officers, posing as fugitive conscientious objectors. They tried to implicate the Fellowship in an intended gaol break, and then in a plot to murder both the Prime Minister and Labour leader Arthur Henderson, for which the leadership of the Derby NCF were sentenced to between five and ten years' imprisonment.

Conscription could finally no longer be avoided, and was brought in through the Military Government Act of January 1916. At first it applied to unmarried men aged 18 to 41 but, by June 1916, it was extended to married men in that age group and, by 1918, to all men up to 51. But, even then, an additional 100,000 people working in what had previously been seen as essential war industries still had to be pressed into military service.

Conscription led to confusion, with many married 'volunteers' under the Derby scheme finding themselves being called up before some unmarried conscripts – the opposite of what Lord Derby had promised. The first Act had to be amended in May to deal with this. However, there were those, like this correspondent, who thought it was quite right for married men without children to take priority for the call-up over those singles who had other family responsibilities:

Is not the case of a young, single man, the mainstay of a widowed mother, or worse still younger brothers, deserving of more sympathy and concessions than the man with a wife only, and in the prime of life?[10]

The list of 'certified occupations' giving exemption continually changed, with the fluctuating and competing demands of the military and the essential industries. In some cases, only men of above a certain age in 'certified occupations' got exemption. Even

Arthur Ravenor – business closure. Business responsibilities were no guarantee of exemption from the call-up.

NOTICE.

IN CONSEQUENCE of the refusal of the Local Tribunal to extend my exemption from Military Service beyond the 16th day of July next, it is my intention to realise the STOCK in TRADE of a PLUMBER and DECORATOR and to DISCONTINUE as from the 22nd day of June next, the BUSINESS formerly carried on at Speenhamland by my Grandfather and my Father, the late Richard Ravenor, and since his death by myself.

ARTHUR STANLEY RAVENOR.

Speenhamland.
May 21st, 1918.

then, it was open to the recruitment officer to argue that a particular individual could be spared from his civilian role for military service. It was not just the nature of one's occupation that could give exemption. The fact that you were the sole proprietor of a family business, on which others depended and for which no alternative proprietor could be found, might also be valid grounds.

In addition to one's occupation, one could claim exemption for personal family responsibilities. Arthur Cook of Alderton seemed to be running a one-man health service, being the sole carer for a blind father, a mentally ill mother and a paralysed brother, though less extreme cases generally tended not to be successful on any long-term basis. The other avenue to exemption was the individual's medical. These were very rigorous at the start of the war, but were progressively relaxed as the need for men became more acute. Many of those rejected at the start of the war were recalled and reassessed. The seven categories (A1 to C3) used at the start of the war were reduced to three:

1. General service – a normal standard of health and strength and capable of enduring the amount of physical exertion appropriate to their age;

2. Those able to stand a fair amount of physical strain and likely to improve if trained. Should be able to march 6 miles and have fair sight and hearing;

3. Not suitable for combatant service, but could be used as auxiliaries (e.g., storekeepers), manual labour or sedentary occupations like clerks.

Some medical conditions were a testament to poverty or neglect; Wiltshire man Albert Blanchard, for example, was only 30, but had no teeth and would have been unable to chew Army biscuits.

Opposition to the war

One factor frequently identified as a cause of the world war was the secret treaties entered into by governments, which dragged nations into hostilities without the consent of their people. Another anti-war organisation, the Union of Democratic Control, was set up to prevent secret diplomacy and it, too, suffered at the hands of more belligerent sectors of the population. Labour politician Ramsay MacDonald was an active player in this and Horatio Bottomley attacked him as a traitor in his mouthpiece magazine *John Bull*. Never one to mince his words, Bottomley added for good measure:

> *We demand his trial by Court martial, his condemnation as an aider and abetter of the King's enemies, and that he be taken to the Tower and shot at dawn.* [11]

If that were not enough, MacDonald's views about the war led to his membership of the Moray Golf Club being rescinded. Bottomley (and the Moray Golf Club) were not alone in trying to do down the Union. The *Daily Express* and the *Daily Sketch* both encouraged their readers to break up the Union meetings and press coverage of these events was anything but neutral:

> *The pacifists are again giving evidence of activity. They have organised another 'peace push' which all British patriots will hastily condemn as mischievous, foolish and ill-advised. Liverpool is already acquainted with these self-appointed*

peacemongers and on the occasion of their last campaign in the city they promptly got the cold shoulder. History now repeats itself . . .

At half past seven some of the 'champions' of the latest 'peace push' put in an appearance near the big lamp in Holt Road. A young lady bobbed up on a chair and proceeded to address an audience numbering about fifty. She had not delivered many sentences before there were indications that the crowd had fully made up their minds not to allow the meeting to proceed . . . At this point, one of the onlookers advanced to the front and his protest against the meeting took the form of quietly lifting the lady from the chair. He argued with her as to the unwisdom of holding the meeting . . . It became apparent that any attempt to continue the proceedings would only lead to trouble. The police were on the scene to carry out their duties in so far as measures of protection were concerned.[12]

Other such meetings prompted more violent disorder:

There were riotous scenes on Plumstead Common on Saturday when Mr. Ramsay MacDonald attempted to hold a meeting under the auspices of the Independent Labour Party and the Woolwich Trades and Labour Council. By 5.30 a crowd of several hundred had gathered on the common, and five minutes later a procession of members of the Royal Woolwich branch of the National Association of Discharged and Demobilised Sailors and Soldiers marched onto the common carrying banners bearing the following inscription – 'All patriots [the Woolwich TLC called itself the Woolwich Patriotic and Labour Council] go to hell with Ramsay MacDonald and his German comrades'. As they approached, there was some cheering and booing . . . The stewards of each party were armed with thick ash sticks and the approach of the discharged soldiers was signalised by a fire of stones, and several of the ILP men were more or less badly injured. Then a rush was made, both parties met and for ten minutes sticks and stones hurtled through the air, and men were carried to the rear, bleeding profusely.[13]

Attempts by MacDonald to re-start the meeting only led to renewed fighting, and the meeting was eventually abandoned, leaving the common littered with stones and broken staves.

The Union (and associated organisations) had 650,000 members by 1917, and its opponents attempted to prove that it was in the pay of the Germans. But investigations revealed that its funds came from the Quakers and from Quaker-owned businesses such as the Cadbury, Fry and Rowntree chocolate manufacturers. When they opened a branch in Oxford, the Union set out a manifesto, which included:

- no territorial change resulting from war to be the product of military force, but rather to be based on the democratic wishes of the population concerned;

- an international council of nations to be set up, replacing 'a balance of power' as a means of regulating international policy;

- no multi-national treaties to be entered into, except by parliamentary consent;

- drastic armaments reductions.

One of the opponents of conscription set out his case in a letter to the local newspaper:

> *The war has been waged so far with a united people; the Government has now decided to finish it with a divided nation. They propose to compel those single men who will not fight as volunteers to fight as conscripts. Thus they are introducing in free England the very Prussianism that we profess to be fighting against.*

The writer went on to argue that the pro-conscriptionists have an ulterior motive of breaking the power of the trades unions and reducing 'the English working man to the position of his docile German confrere'. He continued:

> *We Englishmen have a heritage of individual freedom such is the share of no other nation in Europe. It has been won for us by the suffering and endurance and resolution of our forefathers. It is not a freedom selfishly to please ourselves and we gladly recognise the claim of the state to our loyal services; but we assert too that there is a limit to this claim, and that the prerogative of the individual conscience is higher than that of the state.*[14]

Conscientious objectors

> *God has not put me on this earth to go destroying his children.*

> *Bert Brockleby – conscientious objector, sentenced to death by Lord Kitchener but later reprieved.*

> *I belong to the Independent Labour Party and Socialism is my religion.*

> *Herbert Morrison – First World War conscientious objector and future Home Secretary, addressing the Wandsworth Tribunal*

The idea of conscientious objection had not been legally recognised prior to the First World War, and more specifically before 1916, when conscription was introduced. Until then, and unlike like many European countries, England had relied upon a relatively small volunteer army, underpinned by what was seen as the overwhelming might of the Royal Navy.

Following a campaign by pacifists and their supporters, the 1916 Conscription Act included a 'conscience clause' for conscientious objectors – that is, 'people who object to participation in all forms of war, and whose belief is based on a religious, moral or ethical belief system'. The definition is a much narrower one than that applied in the Second World War. In that later conflict, the Home Secretary for part of the war was Herbert Morrison, who had himself been an objector in the First War, and the grounds for exemption in 1939 were extended to include philosophical and political objections to the conflict. Also, the tribunals in the Second War (led by the Ministry of Labour) attempted to give rather more of a level playing field to the objector, whereas those between 1916 and 1918 (under War Office control) were heavily stacked against them. Over 16,000 went before a tribunal for registration, but only a relative handful was successful.

Objectors could fall into one of three categories. There were *non-combatants*, men prepared to join the military in a non-combatant role. About 3,400 of the applicants signed up for the Non-Combat Corps (or 'No Courage Corps' as sections of the press would have it) or the Royal Army Medical Corps. The remainder were either *alternativists*, prepared to undertake alternative civilian work towards the war effort, or *absolutists*, opposed to doing anything to help the war effort. Some 6,312 people in these last 2 groups were arrested for conscientious objection, of whom 5,970 were court-martialled and some sentenced to death (commuted at the last minute to 10 years' imprisonment).

Others were sent to camps run by the Home Office, to do work that could be variously revolting, back-breaking or pointless, while living in squalor. The Home Office established the Brace Scheme (named after the committee that administered it) to run alternative work schemes. The prisons at Dartmoor and Wakefield were converted into work centres. These were not universally popular with their host populations; Plymouth saw a protest meeting against the Dartmoor centre in April 1917, at which the inmates were accused of harassing local women and of buying up supplies in local shops, and the men were stoned by the locals while on their way to church services. Similar treatment was meted out in the New Forest:

A group of conscientious objectors, who had been sent to work in the New Forest, had a hostile reception on arriving at Brockenhurst. Numbering about sixty, they split up into two parties. One was pelted with clods of turf, booed and hustled, principally by civilians, though some soldiers in the vicinity supplemented their efforts. The other party received rather rougher treatment. Two of their number were ducked in a stream, and their luggage, which was in a lorry, was pitched into the river.[15]

A total of seventy-three objectors died from their treatment, inside or outside of prison. A number became fugitives from the authorities, aided and abetted by an underground network of pacifists, socialists and other sympathisers.

'Conchies', as they became known (with the encouragement of the press), became public pariahs. Not even the postal service was free from 'Conchie-bashing'. One 1916 postcard has them cleaning the trenches with dust-pan and broom, as the bullets whistled round their fighting colleagues. Another shows an effeminate-looking objector in uniform quivering at the point of a beastly Hun's bayonet and saying:

Oh, you naughty unkind German –
Really, if you don't desist
I'll forget I've got a conscience
And I'll smack you on the wrist.

For their part, the anti-conscription movement produced their own postcards, showing what it was really like to be an objector and how they were treated in prison.

But a postcard saved the lives of sixteen objectors in 1916. From the start of the war, the Army introduced the Field Service Post Card (FSPC), a form of censored communication for front-line soldiers, consisting of a number of standard sentences, that the sender could retain or delete, as appropriate. Any additional writing on the card would lead to its destruction by the censors. It was decided in 1916 to make an example of a number of objectors, to encourage the others to join up. As a result, sixteen imprisoned objectors – mainly Quakers and other pacifists, known as the Richmond Sixteen – were moved illegally to Boulogne, where they could be subject to full military discipline and shot. One of them, John Brocklesby, was allowed to send a FSPC home, and he was ingenious with his selective crossing-out, so that the message he sent spelt 'I am being sent down to ... b ... ou ... long ... e'. This gave a clue to his whereabouts; questions were asked in Parliament and the military were forced to return the prisoners to England, where their death sentences were commuted to life imprisonment.

Tribunals

The tribunals to hear claims of conscientious objection were administered locally, including the choice of their members. These were all too often businessmen, shopkeepers, landowners or retired military officers, generally too old to be called up themselves, strongly patriotic and suspicious of anyone who appeared not to be. Apparently, the few female tribunal members that there were tended to be among those most ferociously hostile to conscientious objection. Many of the tribunal members had little understanding of the complicated rules under which they were supposed to operate. One illustration of this came from a man who should have known better. The Birmingham tribunal was chaired by one Neville Chamberlain, then the city's Mayor, and a future Prime Minister. He showed a complete lack of understanding of one applicant's pacifist motivation when he asked: 'You're an accountant; couldn't you go to a munitions factory into the office as an accountant? You'd be paid as an accountant.'

The one member of the tribunal who did know what they were there for was the one appointed to every tribunal by the Army, whose role was to get as many men as possible signed up. Just to add to the ordeal, the would-be conscientious objector could be subject to barracking from a generally hostile public gallery.

By the spring of 1916, conscription was under way in earnest, and the first conscientious objectors (or 'peace cranks' as some in the press chose to call them), started appearing before local tribunals. A crop of twenty-five applications came before one early meeting. The 'religious beliefs' criterion, which was the only one that could justify exemption, seemed to be considerably stretched in some cases, with people claiming to be of the Socialist religion (objecting to the destruction of national brotherhood), Plebeians (not an identifiable group since Roman times?) or adherents to some religious group of their own invention, whose fundamental principle was their non-involvement in warfare. One or two claimed membership of the No-Conscription Fellowship, as if that were a religious organisation, and another claimed that the 'missionary' work he undertook in the suburbs, combined with hospital visits to the war-wounded, was his perfectly adequate contribution to the war effort.

For the most part, conscientious objectors got very short shrift from the tribunals. Even members of more conventional pacifist-religious groups, like the Christadelphians, had a hard time securing complete exemption, particularly where their conversion to pacifism was (in the view of the tribunal) suspiciously recent. But lots of people were getting peace and war mixed up. Even the Swedish government announced that part of the Nobel Peace Prize money was being deducted for Swedish war tax, and would be used by them to purchase weapons of war.

There was scant sympathy for the conscientious objector from the press, as this editorial column shows:

> *One may plead (as a few have done) that his conscience does not allow him to participate in war. He may be reminded that his liberty is only being purchased by the sacrifice and heroism of his brethren. What right has any man, to allow his brethren to purchase his liberty with their blood?[16]*

This editor was at least critical of the conduct of the tribunals:

> *It must be admitted that the action of some tribunals has not been calculated to foster respect and confidence. Members have gone out of their way to browbeat applicants, and in some cases have insulted men whose only crime is that they profess conscientious objection to combatant service. Whatever one may think of the no-fighters who, it seems, are to be drafted into an inglorious non-combatant corps of trench diggers and camp servants, the state has decided to respect individual conscience, and the function of the tribunals is to impartially and judiciously satisfy themselves as to the sincerity of the convictions put forward, and not to adopt hectoring methods, which are totally at variance with the procedure of a court of justice.*

No sympathy for the would-be 'peacemongers', who were characterised as German.

THE KIND OF IRON CROSS FOR PRO-GERMANS.

STAR TREK:
FILM4, 6.55PM

a film of firsts. The first
...le a stand-alone
... overlong telly special, it
...lly, the first not to feature
...m the 1950s TV series. So
...er's Captain Kirk and
...ewart's Jean-Luc Picard
...ion buddies. The plot sees
...arth with the Enterprise
...here's loads of suspense,
...ewart delivering his lines
... majesty. **LI-Z**

...ur TV a smart TV
...th YouView

The Tribunal is not a recruiting agency or a modern 'press gang' but a judicial body with the difficult duty of deciding on the merits of the cases presented to it.[17]

During the summer of 1917 Germany and her allies were floating the idea of a negotiated peace. British opinion was divided, between those who saw it as a heaven-sent opportunity to end the slaughter, and those who saw it as another devilish Hun trick. There was no doubting where this editor's sympathies lay:

The pacifists in this country who talk about a settlement of the war for settlement's sake appear to be of two kinds. There are the Pacifists, whose pro-Germanism is so thinly veiled, and whose aims correspond so nearly with those of the German War Staff, that it is impossible to regard them as British in anything but the accident of birth. There are, secondly, the Pacifists who, though motivated by sincere humanitarian motives and amenable to no charge of conscious treachery, are very plainly the victims and dupes, in many cases, of the former section . . .[18]

The National War Aims Committee held meetings up and down the country, to counter any pacifist weakening of the commitment to wage war. Their meetings heaped doubts on the value of any peace settlement secured without military victory:

It would not be a peace, but simply an armistice, during which the undefeated militarists of Germany would be preparing for the continuance of their war of aggression – for world domination.[19]

But their meetings were not without controversy. In one, the speakers were subjected to constant heckling, and in another, the heckling turned into scuffles and a leading pacifist found himself rather un-pacifically ejected from the hall by stewards. Once order was restored, the meeting unanimously resolved:

To proclaim the nation's inflexible determination to continue the struggle until the evil forces which originated the conflict are destroyed and to maintain the ideals of liberty and justice which are the common and sacred cause of the allies.[20]

None of this deterred one of the cheerleaders of the local pacifists, a Mr Arthur Broadley, from striking up a lively debate in the letter pages of his local newspaper:

With all my soul I condemn the crimes of the German rulers and the part they played in making the war; but I condemn also all the great powers of Europe who in pursuit of precisely the same objects – territory, trade and prestige – have by their secret treaties and alliances plunged innocent workers into fratricidal slaughter. I am convinced that the enemy is not solely responsible for the war, but that dynastic ambitions and quarrels, secret diplomacy, concession hunting, international finance and armament trusts have produced fears, suspicions and needless racial animosities; the result being that the peoples of all the belligerent countries honestly believe that they are fighting a defensive war.[21]

It was a debate in which the editor played a far from neutral role. Having published without comment two longer pieces from correspondents condemning the pacifist stance, he added his own commentary to Mr Broadley's contribution:

> *In these days of shortage of paper we must ask our correspondent to be more brief. It is needless to deal at length with such a hotch-potch of argument and faulty history . . . the greater part of the letter is replete with faulty history . . . If this is the best Mr Broadley can do, candidly, we do not think his letters worth the space they occupy . . . It is impossible to advance discussion with one who perversely ignores well-established and accepted facts.*[22]

After allowing one of Mr Broadley's opponents another chance to blacken his name, the editor declared the correspondence closed.

But even the recruiting authorities could sometimes outreach themselves. The Massey family found themselves bombarded with demands for their son to present himself for military service, despite the fact that he was already serving as a corporal on the Western Front. When he returned home wounded, to recuperate, the authorities promptly arrested him. Neither his uniform nor his evident wounds were apparently enough to persuade them that he was no draft dodger. Another couple in Hull received the call-up papers for their son, and they dutifully reported to the recruiting office, carrying the five-month-old infant concerned. This time, it did not take sharp-eyed officials long to realise that a mistake had been made.

Chapter 5

Tightening your Belts – Rationing

Mary had a little lamb
For little Mary's dinner;
It weighed no more than froth on stout
And that's why Mary's thinner!

Nursery rhyme © 1918, as re-written when rationing was introduced

From the very outset of war the Government recognised that feeding the population was going to be a challenge. To take just two examples, Britain's pre-war policy of free trade had led to a 'grain invasion' from the new world, and the bulk of Britain's pre-war sugar supplies came from Germany. This left the country heavily dependent upon imported foodstuffs, and vulnerable to blockade. Within days of war being declared, the Government gave itself powers to control the retail prices of foodstuffs, and to intervene in other ways if supplies got short. From August 1914, granulated sugar was priced at 4½d a pound, butter 1s 6d a pound, colonial cheese 9½d and bacon 1s 4d or 1s 6d (depending on whether it was Continental or the superior British variety).

Initially, food supplies were not a problem. The prices of luxury foods actually fell, due to people entertaining less, and some dining establishments actually flourished (admittedly at the cost of others):

> *One of the many results of this war is that Manchester has done with German*
> *restaurants, and this opportunity is being taken to emphasise the existence of*
> *some of the city's typically British institutions.[1]*

The advertising feature to which this article was the introduction may speak volumes about the state of British catering in 1914, in that it seemed to want to talk about anything other than the food on offer at the premises being advertised. For one, they focussed on the luxurious nature of the furniture and fittings. Another's main claim to fame appeared to be that they had an all-British staff, and had not employed a foreigner for over ten years. The Merchant's Restaurant boasted that anyone (other than Germans) were welcome to come and inspect their hygienic kitchens at any time, while the Pickwick had an exceptionally well-ventilated smoking room.

It was only when the Germans introduced unrestricted submarine warfare that shortages really began to get serious. Between April and June 1917 over 2 million tons of shipping was lost; prices began to rise steeply (it was estimated that they had doubled since the war began) and there were complaints about profiteering.

Lord Milner, a member of the War Cabinet, made light of the submarine menace in May 1917, but his comments had some unwelcome news for consumers about how the Government intended to respond to it:

> *It is vain to deny that the submarines are the subject of preoccupation in England. It is vainer still to imagine, as do the Germans, that it can force us now or later to make peace ... Whatever happens, we shall be able to preserve the tonnage necessary for food and war material by suppressing the yet considerable quantity of imports and exports not indispensable to the life of the country.* [2]

This newspaper wrung its editorial hands at our apparent inability to defend ourselves from this new menace:

> *It is difficult to see how merchant ships are to protect themselves. It is suggested they should go in groups; that would probably mean a greater loss of life and*

ships and cargoes. Submarines would be a terrible danger to our trade in home
waters if there were more of them . . .³

If people thought the entry of America into the war in 1917 would bring about an immediate transformation of the food situation on the home front, the Director of Food Economy, Sir Arthur Yapp, was quick to disabuse them of the idea:

Although the entry of the United States into the war means much for the Allied
cause, yet every man sent to fight in France under the Stars and Stripes must be
fed and clothed from overseas and this, of course, involves the allocation of a
vast amount of tonnage to the work. Every boatload of food saved on this side of
the Atlantic will release a boat for the service of the soldiers from across the
ocean. We should count 'sacrifice at table as one of the ways by which to
transport America's brave soldiers to the battlefields of Europe'.⁴

Voluntary rationing

The Government were deeply reluctant to introduce compulsory rationing. The public were encouraged instead to limit food consumption by voluntary means:

To conscientiously follow the slight, though very essential, food restrictions, will
help to shorten the war, and it is best to do so voluntarily. To institute a just
system of rationing would need an army of officials that can ill be spared from
other important work. It is, therefore, everyone's duty to make VOLUNTARY food
restrictions a success.⁵

Households who were adhering to the voluntary code of rationing could obtain a card which they could display in their window as an example to others. Buckingham Palace may have had one on display somewhere, since the Royal Family were among the first to sign up to the voluntary code. Its champions rehearsed the arguments for voluntarism (arguments they would soon have to stand on their head):

Unthinking people say: 'If we need to ration, let our rationing be compulsory.
That will make it fair to all'. It will not. With all her organisation, with all the
sheep-like docility of their people, Germany has failed to make it fair to all.
Compulsory rationing in Germany produced bread tickets without producing the
bread, and that brought about serious food riots in the towns. You cannot eat
bread tickets. Compulsory food rationing does not equalise food distributions.
The food sellers become food smugglers, and the rich buy the smuggled food.
The poor get food tickets and perhaps no food.
* Compulsory rationing will waste millions. We might have to print 120 million*
food tickets a week: we might have to find and pay thousands of officials to
distribute them. These officials will have to become spies and spy on food buyers
and food sellers alike. Spying will become a duty . . .
* Our women can save us from compulsory rationing, from spies, more*
registration cards and vast expense. They are on their honour to do it.⁶

Lord Rhondda was appointed Food Controller in the summer of 1917 and immediately appealed for 'every man and every woman to be a Food Controller and every family to be a Vigilance Committee'. But the very idea of appointing a Food Controller was opposed by the Cooperative movement, to the extent that they placed advertisements, asking:

> *Why is it necessary to appoint a Food Controller?*

It was, they said, to prevent unscrupulous dealers from making exorbitant profits by robbing the people. But there was in their view a better solution:

> *Why instead don't the people combine to purchase or produce for themselves and save the dealers' profit?*

Opposition to the rationing scheme, as finally introduced, also came from the Cooperative movement:

> *food rationing, as it was now attempted to be carried on, was a disgrace, and it illustrated the power of capitalism as against the Cooperative movement.*

They called for something more radical:

> *[a] compulsory national scheme of rationing of essential foodstuffs for the purpose of securing a wide and equitable distribution thereon [sic] among all classes of the community and the production of measures which will give consumers' representatives such power to regulate prices as will abolish the opportunities of making exorbitant profits.*[7]

The Government may well have thought that this was precisely what they were doing, when compulsory rationing was finally introduced, but not according to the cooperatives. According to them, the upper classes, as against the masses, had been opposed to food rationing, since it would mean all classes would have to share alike. But:

> *Even now they were not sharing alike. People in the West End of London could still get a good dinner for 5s 6d [27p]. For those who had the money there was no waiting about in queues to get five pennyworth of meat! That was not treating all classes alike, and it was because equal treatment was not being meted out to the people that there was so much dissatisfaction in the country.*[8]

As 1917 moved into 1918 and food shortages got worse, public opinion began to clamour for the fair shares that would come with rationing, and complaints about profiteering were mixed in with some of a decidedly class-war nature, contrasting ordinary people who:

> *had to wait in queues for three or four hours in order to obtain food so that their menfolk and children did not have to want, whereas those in a better position with telephones in their houses had merely to order goods over the telephone and the goods were despatched.*[9]

This editorial took on a rather different class-war tone:

> *We have heard it suggested that it is only the working class that have to go into queues; that people in better circumstances are able to get what they require of the articles which are scarce by ordering it in the usual way . . . that is not so . . .*

the most extravagance in matters of food are [sic] usually to be found in the
homes of the working people, and the working people in the main are the most
disinclined to accommodate themselves to new circumstances . . .[10]

As it became ever harder to obtain food, and eventually even the well-to-do were being forced to line up with everybody else, it appeared that hostilities in the queues were forcing some women to go shopping in disguise:

Women with good incomes, compelled by the food shortage to go 'foraging' have
found it undesirable, says the Daily Graphic, when joining a queue to wear
clothes conveying any suggestion of opulence. The sarcastic comments of the
other women in the queues have not been pleasant. So garments which in other
circumstances would be referred to as 'my old rags' are worn for the occasion.
The only obviously 'fashionable' people to be seen in the queues are prosperous
munitions girls. They could not appear in public without one of those wonderful
fur coats![11]

In January 1918, workers in Manchester staged a hunger march in protest against the food shortages and queuing. It coincided with the announcement that a food rationing scheme, aimed at addressing many of their concerns, would come into effect in March. A crowd of between 4,000 and 5,000 assembled in Albert Square, in an atmosphere that was described as 'good-natured but determined'. Speakers told of working men coming home after a day of toil to a dinner of bread and jam, their wives in tears after a day of futile queuing. There was a widely held belief (denied by the authorities) that 'cold-air' stores around Manchester were piled high with food, being held back by speculators seeking to create shortages. Rationing was welcomed, but only if Lord Rhondda supplied the city with the food needed for its population.

One possible solution to the food problem was the introduction of communal kitchens, as part of the national food-saving campaign. Right at the start of the war, it was recognised that some families would be plunged into hardship by the departure of the breadwinner, and the Portsmouth Soup Kitchen offered to provide such families with up to 600 gallons of food (their repertoire was not limited to soup) a day. But now the idea was to be widened:

Food is unquestionably the most important question of the hour, and the coming
of the Communal Kitchen must be welcome to thousands of harassed
housewives. The term applied to these wartime institutions may deter many from
patronising them, since it savours somewhat of the soup kitchen, but common
sense should overcome this objection. Experience has proved that the Communal
Kitchen effects a great saving of time and labour devoted to the preparation of
meals. Domestic and shopping difficulties have largely increased the demand for
ready-cooked food. Much time has now to be spent on marketing – often to very
little purpose – and a makeshift meal with ready-cooked food sometimes offers
the best solution. All of which is paving the way for Communal Kitchens for all
classes.[12]

Reading opened one in September 1917 and, perhaps surprisingly:

*among those who availed themselves of the Kitchen's varied and wholesome bill
of fare were many people who obviously belonged to the middle class section of
the community . . .*[13]

One possible explanation for these kitchens' popularity among the 'middle class section
of the community' might be the mass exodus of domestic staff (including cooks) into
better paid and more patriotic (not to say more liberating) work in the war economy. The
middle classes now had not only to queue for the food but also prepare it, apparently
with marked effects on their eating habits:

*So many of us now do our own cooking that ordering meals, instead of being a
consultation with the cook, is an argument with ourselves.*[14]
*In the middle-class home the difficulty of obtaining servants, or even a woman
who can render a few hours' help, has tended enormously to the simplification of
meals. There are houses at the present time
which have fused afternoon tea and
dinner into the 'high tea' of early
Victorian habits. It is a practical
compromise that makes for
economy in various and
obvious directions, and not
least of its recommendations
is that it diminishes the
washing-up required.*[15]

How to cook – austerity style

Food economy exhibitions
became the order of the day. An
advertisement for one such
promised substitutes for wheat,
sugar and potatoes and a wealth of
good ideas for a wholesome
meatless dinner costing less than
8*d*. The joys of pulses, roots and
nuts featured large and there was
to be a reading of a proclamation
from the King, calling for
abstention from all unnecessary
grain consumption. The Ministry
of Food sent out demonstrators, to
give 'practical advice in the use of
available foods, with a view to
making them palatable and

Meatless days – part of
the attempt to make
voluntary rationing work.

obtaining from them the maximum amount of value'. But this department store took abstention to a gourmet level:

> *Heelas have secured the eminent services of Mr Eustace Miles M.A., the most prominent exponent of meatless foods, and a lecture, to be followed by a demonstration in meatless cookery will be given in their restaurant on Thursday next.*[16]

One item that certainly was not in short supply, to judge from the recipes being issued by the Ministry of Food as rationing was being introduced, was potatoes. People were encouraged to make potato and oatmeal soup, curried potatoes, potato cakes, or this recipe for:

> *Potato and Macaroni Pudding:*
>
> *Ingredients: 2 oz macaroni, 8 oz mashed potato, 4 oz flour, 2 oz fat (suet or margarine), one dried egg, 2 oz peanuts (baked for 10 minutes), seasoning, a little spice, a little of the water in which the macaroni has been boiled to make a soft mixture.*
>
> *Break the macaroni into 1 inch lengths and boil until tender in salted water. Chop up the suet and baked nuts very finely and add all the ingredients together, binding with one egg. Pour into a greased tin and steam for 1 or 1¼ hours. Turn out and serve with a good brown sauce, in which some piquant sauce has been added.*[17]

But surely even the Ministry could have come up with a better name for another of its recipes than 'Delicious soup made of ingredients usually thrown away'? (In case you were thinking of trying it, its main ingredients were vegetable peelings and cheese rinds.) With regard to this particular recipe, the Ministry were beaten to it by the aforementioned prominent exponent of meatless foods Eustace Miles. Anticipating at the very start of the war that the poor would have a difficult time feeding themselves, Mr Miles called upon his fellow citizens to boil up their vegetable peelings and other waste products into a nourishing soup, which could then be distributed among the poor. His soup would be served with a generous helping of gratuitous advice:

> *I wish also that a few leaflets could be scattered broadcast among the poor, advising them to masticate foods [chew soup?] more thoroughly (and thus lessen the bulk needed) and practice gentle but deep and full breathing and keep the blood clean by sipping hot or cold water first thing in the morning or last thing at night. Our people will need not only all the cheap food but also all the cheap health that can be had.*[18]

Despite the shortages, the throwing of rice at weddings was not banned until later in the war, and reports came in from Aigburth that groups of youths were going round the churchyard, picking up individual grains of rice to feed their chickens.

Hoarding

Even before rationing came in, regulations were enacted, outlawing the hoarding of foodstuffs. Article 1 of the Food Hoarding Order 1917 stated that:

No person shall after the 19 April 1917 acquire any article of food so that the quantity of such article in his possession or under his control at any one time exceeds the quantity required for ordinary use or consumption.

But what constituted hoarding? The Regulation itself was unclear and those who looked to official sources for guidance looked in vain. One Ministry official said that it was almost impossible to lay down a hard and fast rule; another speculated that a two- to three-week supply of staple items would not be deemed excessive, while yet another thought a month's worth of stores was acceptable. Just to complicate matters further, another suggested that it all depended on where you lived, with people in remote locations being allowed more leeway than others, and the public was also told that home-produced foodstuffs like jam and chutney did not count.

Basingstoke first tested out the Regulations in January 1918, when the authorities (very probably aided by a tip-off from a malicious neighbour) raided the home of a Mr Richard Rowell. Mrs Rowell claimed to have just minimal quantities of what were going to be rationed foodstuffs, but a search of her house and a garden shed yielded 3lb 11oz of tea, 18lb of sugar and 3lb of margarine. This was evidently enough to breach the rules, since the lot was confiscated, leaving them with nothing to eat and a 30*s* (£1.50) fine to pay. A rather more unambiguous breach of the regulations came to light when a search of a Mrs Dora Gadesden's home yielded no less than 551lb of bacon and ham. Admiral Sir Richard Poore must have thought he was still catering for the crew of a dreadnought, for he was found to possess a larder whose contents weighed in at around ¼ ton. He said in his defence that his wife had been taken ill, and that he had stepped in

The Director of Food Economy's Appeal

In 1914 the need was for **MEN**
In 1915 for **MUNITIONS**
In 1916 for **MONEY**
In 1917 for **MEN MUNITIONS · MONEY**

and Economy in Food

Arthur R. Yapp.

More economy in food is needed, if rationing is to be avoided.

(inexpertly) to look after the domestic catering. It cost him a £30 fine and the confiscation of most of his food.

An Amnesty Week was declared in February 1918, offering people the opportunity to declare and yield up any secret hoards without fear of prosecution.

Central regulation – and its consequences

Interference in the market could have all sorts of unintended consequences. By allowing the prices of fruit and vegetables to rise substantially, relative to other foodstuffs, the authorities contributed to a fall in their consumption to well below the levels that would be recommended for good health today. A high price for beef, relative to dairy products, could encourage farmers to send their dairy cattle for slaughter, contributing to a future shortage of dairy products. The appeal to the British public to eat less meat – reducing consumption to 2½lb per person per week – actually worked, reducing consumption by 20–30 per cent. But it also had the effect of putting almost 3,000 butchers out of business in short order. While their sales dropped correspondingly, their overheads in many cases increased, due to the war. Butchers also reported another disturbing development among their more affluent customers – it seems that those who habitually bought the choicest cuts of meat had been trading down. The consequence of this was a shortage of the less desirable bits of the animal for the common people to buy. A spokesman for the trade said:

> *One cannot but hope that the wealthier class will be patriotic enough to return to their accustomed joints, and thus allow the supply to become normal again.*[19]

Even the pupils at Eton College had some adjustments to their diet, though it is questionable whether it could be described as austerity:

> *Owing to the meat shortage, the boys at Eton College are being supplied with venison from Windsor Great Park, a number of royal bucks having been purchased by a local butcher.*[20]

The coming of compulsory rationing

Sugar was the first foodstuff to be subject to rationing. The Government's initial idea was simply to give every retailer 50 per cent of the amount they had received in 1915 and let them ration it out as they saw fit. This did not work, not least because of the massive movements in population, due to the war economy. They then went for a system based on registering the number of households the

MEAT RATIONING

———◆———

O'HARA & LEE BROTHERS,
BUTCHERS,
HENLEY-ON-THAMES,
Wargrave, Nettlebed and Hambleden,

Beg to state that they are not responsible for the Quality of the Meat sold in any of their establishments. –

Under the Rationing Scheme they are obliged to sell the Meat allotted to them, whatever its quality may be.

The buying is taken entirely out of their hands.

———————————————

Meat rationing. This butcher despairs of the rationing scheme.

retailer served, but again this did not take account of individuals shifting from one household to another. Eventually, a system of registering each individual had to be introduced, which became the model for all rationing, in this war and the next.

Rationing was highly devolved; some 1800 local Food Control Committees were responsible for setting maximum prices, registering their local population (a national register was started but never finished) and setting up a rationing scheme (or not, as they decided). This created an odd situation in which one area could have its own rationing system, while its next-door neighbour had a different one, or none at all. But, for all its anomalies, the system worked. In London and the Home Counties (where the authorities did manage to establish a common scheme serving some 10 million people) the Metropolitan Police estimated that the number of people queuing for food fell from 1.3 million to less than 7,000 within a month of its introduction. Most of those residual queues were thought to be for non-rationed goods.

Nonetheless, it proved to be a major challenge just to get people to fill in the application forms for ration cards correctly. One argument revolved around an obscure debate as to whether 'married woman' constituted an occupation. Mr Herbert Pretty certainly thought so when he filled out his wife's details. When the form was returned marked 'incomplete', he was sufficiently angered to send an open letter to the Local Food Control Committee, which his local paper published. In it, he said:

As rationing starts to be introduced, grocers compete to get people to register with them.

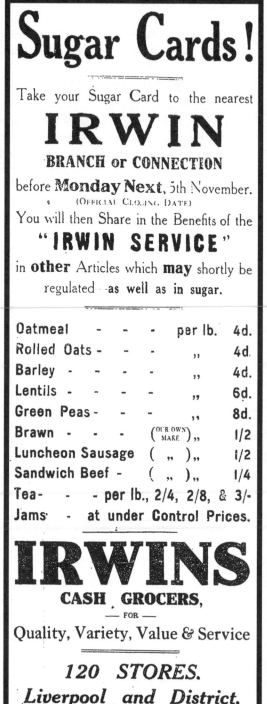

It is generally assumed that a married woman's occupation is that of looking after her household and I am told that throughout the country this designation is regarded as adequate.

I return the form, on which I have stated the various self-imposed duties that my wife, in common with most English women, is performing in aid of our fighting forces and the allies.[21]

This occasioned a long reply from the Local Food Control Committee, in which they patiently explained that 'married woman' was a state, not an occupation, especially at a time when so many married women followed a definite calling as part of the war economy. It transpired that one reason why people's occupations were needed on the form was to ensure they got the right rations. People doing heavy manual work could expect more of certain rations than those in sedentary jobs. We were not told into which category 'married woman' fell.

The issue of ration cards seemed to be fraught with wider problems. There were delays in printing them, due to a paper shortage; many applicants (no doubt unfamiliar with the bureaucratic process) failed to fill in the paperwork correctly, or on time; and the individual retailers who issued them seemed to take forever to do so. Then so many people lost theirs that the authorities decided to introduce a fine for those seeking replacements. Each week, the newspaper would carry details of how much the housewife could expect in her ration for the coming week, and each week it seemed from the notice that this or that commodity would be in short supply or was entirely unavailable, or that some shops may experience local shortages. Workers who spent part of their working week away from their home town reported great difficulty in obtaining their allowances. The rationing arrangements were far from being a smoothly oiled machine.

Other people's rationing

Britain was not alone in imposing rationing, and the merits (or otherwise) of different nations' schemes became the subject of propaganda. The shortcomings of the German scheme were one of the arguments used against introducing compulsory rationing in Britain. It was argued that the German system did not properly control the distribution of food. It issued everybody with tickets, adding up to the amount of food nationally available, but did nothing to stop the wealthy buying up supplies on the black market, leaving the poor with nothing to eat but food tickets.

But, according to the German press (if one were to believe the second-hand accounts of it in the English newspapers) there was precious little food left in Britain to be rationed. German readers were being told that Sunday lunch in Britain now consisted of just two courses – potato peelings and cheese rind (better known, as we saw, as 'Delicious soup made of ingredients usually thrown away'). In similar (but rather more obviously comical) vein, British readers were being told that the Germans were now reduced to two suits of clothing – one made of cardboard and another of blotting paper, for when it rained. Of more immediate concern to many Germans would be the fact that they apparently had a serious shortage of tobacco. They were bulking out their supplies by adulterating it with old hops or the leaves of sycamore, beech and other trees. The Austrians were said to market hops as 'Hindenburg Tobacco Substitute', though it speaks volumes for the effects of these substitutes that it was forbidden to send them to soldiers serving at the front.

In case anyone was still feeling bad about the privations of the British rationing system, this local paper, as part of its anti-Bolshevik campaign, gave its readers a taste of what the cost of eating was like under the ironically named 'Peace with Plenty' regime the new Russian government had promised. For reference, a rouble was then worth 2*s* 1d (just over 10p):

> *A pound of bad, black bread, bought without cards, costs between 10 and 12 roubles. The bread bought with cards (a quarter of a pound per diem, when any is available at all) is almost uneatable. Potatoes are 2 roubles a pound. Rice is unobtainable, even at 15 roubles a pound. Sugar is 23 roubles, beef 10 to 12 roubles, a bottle of wine at a restaurant 150 roubles and cognac 500 roubles. The railway buffets contain nothing but hot water.[22]*

The humour of rationing

And so, step by step, rationing was introduced to First World War Britain. The British dealt with it, as they dealt with most privations, by grumbling and by making jokes about it:

> *Please Mummy, Billy and me's playing shops and we've used up all your coupons. May we have some more?*

> *When the charlady turned up to do her half day, the mistress was a little disconcerted by her smile of welcome. 'Why, Eliza,' she said 'What have you done with your teeth?' 'Well, mum,' replied the charlady 'we ain't goin' to 'ave anythin' to chew until the war's over, so I've pawned them'.[23]*

Chapter 6

Women and the War

The war would fundamentally change the role of women in the economy, and in society. At the outbreak of hostilities, we were given some insights into a contemporary view of women, as the weaker vessels. At the speech day for Pendleton High School for Girls, Headmistress Miss R. Patterson offered these thoughts on the character of the modern English girl:

> *Girls nowadays develop a sense of responsibility much later than formerly, which made it necessary that they should receive an education of reasonable length and consecutiveness. The girls who went to the Pendleton School were of the class that should not leave until they reached the age of seventeen years. It was not sufficient that they should finish their education at fifteen to go home and be generally useful . . . There was a tendency among some young girls to go to picture palaces, bazaars and garden parties with the result that they expended a good deal of energy and lost regularity of habits. There was too much striving after pleasure and for the individual to develop herself at the expense of others.[1]*

These last thoughts were echoed by a Miss Burstall, the Headmistress of Manchester High School, who warned her parents against allowing their daughters to walk the promenades and attend variety entertainments while on holiday, since:

> *Such constant excitement to girls was harmful, and far more exhausting than school work.[2]*

But it seems the girls had more sterling qualities than their headmistresses gave them credit for. By 1915, the Manchester High School speech day heard that the girls had manufactured thousands of respirators for soldiers, along with 8,000 other useful articles and no less than 2,500lb of jam. Sixth-form science students were engaged in Government work and many former pupils were helping out at military hospitals – all of this without harming the school's academic record.

Some 80,000 English women would serve in non-combatant roles in the armed forces. Many more entered the war economy in one way or another, either manufacturing war materials or filling the vacancies left by the men who had joined up. By 1918 about a million were working in munitions or engineering alone, and another 260,000 in the Women's Land Army.

Women in the war economy

About 1.6 million women entered the war economy between 1914 and 1918. About half of them went into manufacturing, often taking on jobs previously considered too physically or mentally demanding or unpleasant for the fairer sex. But some 400,000 also went into commercial and financial work (a sector particularly affected by Army recruitment). At the start of the war, there were those who saw women's wartime role as the traditional one, of tearfully waving their menfolk off to war and keeping the home fires burning. The following meeting was representative of that view.

The meeting at the Town Hall promised to tell the girls in the audience how they could best help the nation in its hour of need. But anyone hoping to hear about munitions work or nursing the troops would be in for a disappointment. The Countess Ferrers talked mostly about her recently-founded League of Honour, which seemed mainly to involve making a pledge of prayer, purity and temperance. The Countess Gurowslea sought to inspire the audience with the profound insight 'ever follow that which is good' and the meeting ended with the singing of 'Oh God, our help in ages past'.

Of rather more practical use, in a Girl Guide-ish sort of way, was a meeting of the Woman's Volunteer Corps:

> *It was not a fierce band of women going about shooting and doing everything masculine, but they aimed at general utility and general competence – that women should be collected into corps to learn everything likely to be of service to them and to the community. They were being taught signalling, telegraphy, nursing, cooking, first aid and other things. They were arranging for camps, and their aim was to do the best they could, on the principle of the Boy Scouts with their badges, etc. Women no doubt ought to know how to shoot, in order to defend themselves, but while every woman ought to be armed they must wait until they received orders.[3]*

Domestic service was the traditional employment for much of the female labour force, and in Oxford in July 1914 the readership of the local paper appeared to be more concerned about the servant problem than the approaching war:

> *One hears so much in these days about the servant problem that it sets one thinking and wishing for an improvement. Why is it that the demand is so much larger than the supply? I feel sure the answer to that is that there is no honest, hard-working group of women so looked down on and spoken so sneeringly of as the domestic servant.'*

The correspondent, who signed her(?)self 'An old servant of forty years' standing' goes on to compare their lot unfavourably with that of a shop assistant, despite the fact that, in her view, 'a gentleman's house is a little higher than a shop'.[4]

This provoked a lively correspondence. One respondent thought she had the answer:

> *No doubt some servants are not respectable; neither do they care a toss-up about their work. But still there are good girls in this profession, and many more would be forthcoming if employers made service more pleasant and respected them. They require machines that will keep going from morning to night. Servants should be given the same considerations of liberty etc. as the shop girls, and why not call them 'Miss'? They are entitled to it.[5]*

The war economy left many mistresses servantless and created a market for labour-saving products.

This correspondent went on to explain that modern girls were more enlightened, having had the benefit of the council schools, and would not be willing to tolerate the humiliations traditionally associated with service. What none of them knew was that the servant shortage was about to get a whole lot worse.

As the killing fields of the Western Front drew more and more men out of the domestic economy, the authorities were increasingly forced to look to women to take on unfamiliar roles to fill the gaps. By March 1917, the Queen, no less, was leading the call to women to do more for the war effort:

The Queen gave the encouragement not only of her approval, but of her presence in a time of personal mourning to the great meeting at the Albert Hall in London, at which the representatives of the government issued their appeal to the women of these islands to give further help to the country's cause . . . Never in the history of humanity has there been a finer indication of the moral and spiritual grandeur of womanhood than that which the daughters of Britain have effected in the hour of trial. The sympathy, the alacrity, the courage, the labour, the skill of women have given a response beyond praise to the innumerable calls of the nation's needs . . .

the huge military requirements of the war have established conditions that make systematic national service for the civilian population absolutely needful and the preponderant part of the civilian population now consists of women.[6]

Early in the war, the Queen had even launched a fund:

In the firm belief that the prevention of distress is better than its relief, and that employment is better than charity, I have inaugurated the Queen's 'Work for Women' fund. Its object is to provide employment for as many as possible of the women of this country who have been thrown out of work by the war.

I appeal to the women of Great Britain to help their less fortunate sisters through this fund.

Mary R.[7]

But what could women actually do? New opportunities for women raised some quaintly paternalistic concerns in the Home Office. For while, in their view, war brought out the best in men, it had the opposite effect on women. For men, the disregard for material wellbeing combined with exceptional circumstances made the influence of bodies like the YMCA and the Church Army very real and effective. But for women, the deadening and unnerving monotony of factory life added, in many instances, to a largely developed earning capacity, led to the development of a materialistic outlook.

But no fears of deadening and unnerving monotony should have worried the 500 'educated girls' being recruited as Marconi wireless mechanics:

A knowledge of mathematics is essential, as the operations are extremely delicate and subtle. This is no blind alley occupation, for it leads to a well-paid career for life . . . The educated girl often hesitates to volunteer for work in a munition or aircraft factory, because she fears the grimness and monotony of the toil and contact with the rough, uncouth 'hands'. But the war has revolutionised the factory, as it has our daily life. The vast hives of industry that have sprung up like mushrooms all over the land are perfect workshops, equipped with marvellous machines, and the 'hands' are as often women of the highest culture and education as the one-time untaught, illiterate factory girl.[8]

Marconi may have wanted educated women, but they were not universally prized:

> *Clever women are looked upon with suspicion, especially by the pious. That is*
> *why so many people write 'be good, sweet maid, and let who can be clever' in*
> *autograph albums; they flatter themselves that there is a real, if hidden, affinity*
> *between virtue and stupidity.[9]*

Apparently to their amazement, even the Ministry of Munitions discovered that women were capable of skilled work:

The Ministry of Munitions is extending its plans for the employment of women in engineering work involving a considerable amount of skill in order to replace manpower withdrawn for the army. It has been found that educated women are capable of undertaking this more skilled work and the Ministry appeals to such women to come forward and offer themselves for this service.[10]

One of the opportunities for the female labour force was agriculture. A campaign had been launched to recruit 100,000 female farm-workers, though its promoters did not seem exactly sure whether women, clever or otherwise, were up to the task:

Various organisations have been formed to promote the movement, and some of them have produced excellent results, but it has yet to be proved that women have the physical strength, and that they can be organised and trained in large numbers to undertake a considerable part of the agricultural work of the country.[11]

But it was not just their physical strength and their ability to be organised that had the Government concerned. If the grimness and monotony of industrial toil was considered un-ladylike, they equally feared that a life of healthy outdoor physical labour might in some way undermine their femininity. The Government issued lady agricultural recruits with this stern warning:

You are doing a man's work and so you are dressed rather like a man; but remember that because you wear a smock and trousers you should take care to behave like an English girl who expects chivalry and respect from everyone she meets.

One career at least was forcing women to abandon ladylike behaviour. The disappearance of so many stable-boys to the front meant that racing stables were having to employ stable girls. The trainers spoke highly of them but the female tradition of riding side-saddle was not really suited to race horses, and they were forced to go astride.

The ideal of a demure English rose did not tally with the experience of this correspondent:

Everyone will admit that women are doing their utmost at this critical time and are deserving of the greatest praise, but, one regrets to have to say it, there are many instances of offhandedness and rudeness on the part of some of them, especially to others of their own sex . . . They treated customers far worse than men ever did. When one woman asked for margarine, the girl shook her head. The woman repeated the question whether they had margarine and the girl rejoined 'Can't you read?'[12]

The correspondent went on to cite cases of rudeness involving telephone operators and tram conductresses, and another wrote in to add post office counter staff to the list. This latter provoked a lively correspondence, some of it conducted in verse, in which the additional burdens loaded onto post offices by the war, and the stupidity of the general public were prayed in aid. By contrast, this correspondent felt that the advent of women tram conductresses had improved the behaviour of the passengers:

The advent of women into this particular sphere of activity tends to improve the manners of the travelling public. People are more anxious to avoid giving the girl official unnecessary trouble, more ready to oblige others, while they always come to the assistance of the woman conductor who may have a refractory or garrulous passenger to deal with.[13]

There was also resistance to women agricultural workers from traditionalists among the farming community. One official tried to overcome this by threatening the farmers with the importation of 'foreigners':

At St Michael's Parish Hall, Miss Bradley, Agricultural Organising Officer for the Board of Trade said that Sussex had been one of the best counties for recruiting the army and navy, and she hoped with the cooperation of the farmers it would occupy a similar position with regard to women working on the land and filling the places of the men who had gone to fight for their country. She knew that in Sussex there was a strong feeling against 'foreigners' and therefore it was all the more necessary that women of Sussex should help in this movement, so that it would not be necessary to import female labour from other counties . . . Women generally had responded splendidly to this call for service. The same could not hardly be said of the farmers, but she realised there were difficulties and prejudices were gradually being overcome, and that when farmers realised that women could do useful work they would accept their service more and more readily. Women were proving in many directions that they could perform useful work . . . On farms, too, they could be of great assistance – they could do valuable work with weeding. Three pence an hour was the minimum wage for untrained helpers.[14]

If the threat of female labour from neighbouring counties could leave Sussex farmers feeling threatened, what would they make of the Government's other alternative? This took the form of 10,000 Germans (prisoners of war and interned resident aliens) with skills in agriculture. This last measure gave rise to fears that Huns were to be billeted on agricultural labourers. The authorities were at pains to say that this was not the case, and that they would be returned to a 'central depot' at the end of the working day. Allied soldiers with agricultural skills were made available to British farmers during the main cultivating season, and it had been planned to release 30,000 for that purpose during the 1918 season. But a rather more pressing demand on their time came up, in the form of the last great German offensive. The Women's War Agricultural Committees were called upon to make up the shortfall (whether the farmers liked it or not).

Women may have been doing men's work, but not necessarily for men's rates of pay, and this upset one group of male workers. Disabled ex-soldiers seeking light civilian employment complained that the work was being monopolised by women, earning less than the male rate for the job. Such jobs as were available only provided a living wage if they could be eked out, for example by a military service pension.

Manchester City Council provoked a two-day strike of its male tramway staff by daring to propose appointing women tramcar inspectors. The staff complained that there were sufficient men, not eligible for the call-up, to do the job, and that the women were

International Stores bring in a small army of women to man the empty shop counters.

being paid less than male inspectors. For their part the company explained that a growing number of women tram conductors were being appointed and that, in their view, women should only be supervised by women. They gave an undertaking that female inspectors would only be used on trams with female conductors.

The demonisation of the alien population seems to have created new job opportunities for British women workers:

> *Before the war the craft of the hairdresser, like many other industries, was almost entirely in the hands of foreigners, but the alien has now been practically eliminated and the skilled woman hairdresser is coming to the fore.*[15]

With all these new avenues for female employment opening up, nursing was having difficulty in recruiting enough new staff. In particular, members of the Voluntary Aid Detachments, who had actual experience in nursing wounded military men, were showing little inclination to move over into mainstream nursing. In case anyone wondered why this might be, the union that was supposed to champion the profession's interests offered this disturbing indictment of the job:

> *The National Union of Trained Nurses gives a number of reasons why the right woman is seeking other occupations that offer greater advantages. First and foremost, the work is unreasonably hard whilst the prospects are of the poorest. The hours are too long and the holidays too infrequent and short. No provision is made for preparation for examinations, which has to be done during the off-duty hours. The time for meals is all too short, and the food all too often of inferior quality and badly cooked. Training is not completed until the nurse has attained her twenty-fifth year and she is considered too old at forty. Little wonder then that the VAD who has had valuable experience in hospitals declines to become a trained nurse.*[16]

Small wonder, then, that by 1918 a £250,000 appeal had been launched, to set up a Nation's Fund for Nurses. Its aims were to establish and maintain a college of nursing and to establish a benevolent fund for the profession. The promoters reiterated many of the complaints of the nurses themselves; they had no state register, no centralised organisation to regulate and safeguard the interests of their profession, no general entrance examination, no minimum number of hours for lecture and study during training, no uniform curriculum or qualifying examination and no centralised benevolent fund or pension scheme, though their work was most strenuous and their working life necessarily short.

Some women simply devoted themselves to the traditional role of supporting our boys at the front – not always, it seemed, with conspicuous success:

> *Some of the ladies who have volunteered to make garments for our troops are said to have very crude ideas of needlework and cutting out, which only emphasises the action of those who claim that the work should be done by women who are regularly engaged in the making of wearing apparel. One paper states that one of the shirts made by an enthusiastic amateur measured about six feet square. It might have come in handy as a bell tent.*[17]

They had no excuse, for the Red Cross had issued patterns for making garments for the war wounded and their carers, including such items as nurse's aprons, surgeon's overalls, bed jackets, sleeping suits and a garment beguilingly named the 'helpless case shirt'.

By 1918, there were even fears that women would be conscripted into the armed forces. The Reading Chamber of Commerce had reports from its members that female employees were quitting their jobs and going into munitions production, for fear that they might otherwise be conscripted. The Chamber sought, and got, reassurance from the Government that there were no such plans.

With there being no call for female aircrew in the Royal Flying Corps, perhaps the nearest a woman got to a career in the skies was Lily Druce, a former office window cleaner in Manchester:

> *The girl steeplejack has now made her appearance – another war product. An Evening Chronicle representative today discovered a small crowd of city men looking skywards in admiration and awe. Attention was riveted on a twenty-year-old girl walking a ten inch plank 120 feet from the ground. The plank was bending rather ominously with every step, and spectators looked in with almost breathless excitement as the girl steeplejack, apparently oblivious of danger, proceeded to 'point' the wall of a huge warehouse.*
>
> *Conscious of the attentions from below, this girl hero – for men steeplejacks have hitherto been regarded as something approaching heroes – caused a ripple of laughter by singing a merry 'Good-by-eee'.*
>
> *'That's the limit' exclaimed an elderly gentleman in a tall hat.*[18]

She may have been attracted by the excitement of the job, but more likely by the £3 a week starting wage, and her employer was so pleased with her performance that he was keen to recruit other 'steeple-jills'.

Perhaps the authorities were missing a trick in not giving women a more active role in the armed services. For, if the thought of hordes of militant suffragettes gave some Englishmen nightmares, they apparently had the same effect on the Germans. Interrogations of several German prisoners of war revealed the same fear, set out in a letter one of them was carrying:

> *Several battalions of suffragettes have landed at Havre. There are 500 women in each battalion. I want to warn you to be very careful when you meet them. Don't let them scratch out your eyes, and, above all, don't let them capture you. That would shame you before the whole world.*[19]

But one woman at least made a more radical attempt to pursue a military career:

> *Elizabeth Ishmael, a girl of twenty employed as a domestic servant at Leyton, fired by stories of girls joining the army as boys, tried to follow their example. On her afternoon off she proceeded to London, where she induced a barber to cut her hair on the plea that this was in accordance with a doctor's orders. She then purchased a suit of clothes 'for her brother' and eventually went to Uxbridge.*
>
> *On the journey she learned that she would have to be medically examined, a*

Crowds outside Buckingham Palace cheer the King, Queen and Prince of Wales, as war is declared in August 1914. (IWM Q 81832)

Bomb damage in Eltham, Kent, following an air raid. (HO 92)

The pilot of this Farman biplane chose slightly too small a field for his emergency landing in 1915. Police are on hand to deter souvenir hunters. (RBC 1395145)

Cavalrymen and their horses gather for embarkation to France in August 1914. (RBC 1314828)

Recruits for the Royal Engineers leave for their training camp near Ripon in July 1915. Their regiment would see action in most of the great battles of the war. (RBC 1266957)

Food shortages led to serious problems with queuing (this example is in Reading) prior to the introduction of rationing in 1918. (IWM Q 56276)

Girl Guides tend their allotment during the First World War. (IWM Q 27919)

Women operate cranes in a munitions factory at Chilwell, Nottingham. (IWM Q 30038)

A posed propaganda photograph, showing a member of the Sherwood Foresters (the Nottinghamshire and Derbyshire Regiment) being greeted by his mother on his return home on leave. (IWM Q 30402)

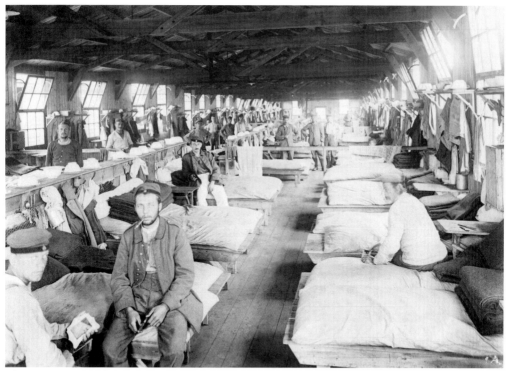

Sleeping quarters for German prisoners of war at Eastcote camp, Northamptonshire (also known as Pattishall). (IWM Q 64122)

Female munitions workers attend the funeral of a colleague in Swansea, killed in a work accident in August 1917. (IWM Q 108452)

Even schoolchildren are enlisted into the war effort. They are seen here making aids for wounded soldiers. (RBC 1267225)

Loyal crowds assemble to welcome the King and Queen, as they visit a war hospital in Reading, July 1915. (RBC 1371119)

Up and down the country women were recruited as tram conductresses, as their male counterparts enlisted. (RBC 1244277)

A tank in Trafalgar Square in November or December 1917 – part of the War Bonds fund-raising appeal. (IWM Q30333)

Here at last! American troops parade down Piccadilly. (IWM Q 53994)

Parades up and down the country marked the Armistice in November 1918. (RBC 1247479)

difficulty she had not foreseen. She then went to Stoke Poges where, in a shrubbery, she changed into male attire. As she was overtaken by a storm she called at a house at Stoke Poges, where she confessed and the Slough Police were communicated with. The girl's mother and her late mistress were informed of the occurrence and on Tuesday afternoon Mr A.C. Thompson, the Police Court Missionary at Slough, took her to her home.[20]

Votes for women

Another group of women for whom the war brought a change of fortunes was the suffragists. The National Union of Women's Suffrage Societies announced at the outset of the war that it was suspending its normal political activities for the duration and devoting itself instead to war relief work. Even the militant suffragettes put their campaigns on hold and many became (sometimes ferociously) patriotic (though a few supported conscientious objection and some helped shelter pacifist deserters).

The Society wasted no time in articulating its views. In September 1914, it called for the opportunity:

To set free for military service the thousands of men engaged in such occupations as ticket clerks, omnibus conductors, salesmen in drapery and provision shops, etc. whose places could be taken effectively by women. In every case where possible, preference should be given to the relatives of the men who enlist. The substitution is to be strictly temporary, i.e. there must be no idea of women snatching an industrial advantage for themselves out of the national need.[21]

There was an early added bonus for the suffragettes, when the Home Secretary told the House of Commons within weeks of the outbreak of war:

I have advised his Majesty to remit the remainder of the sentences of all persons now undergoing terms of imprisonment for activities connected with the suffrage agitation. This has been undertaken without solicitation on their part and without requiring any undertaking from them.[22]

The female contribution to the war effort helped to persuade many, from former Prime Minister Asquith down, that they should be given the right to vote. This passed through the House of Commons in December 1917, and into law in June 1918, though not everyone – including this correspondent, signing himself 'Citizen' – was persuaded of the case:

We have a right to expect that the Government will devote all its powers to the prosecution of the war, and not fritter them away on matters which have nothing to do with victory. Because numbers of women are behaving splendidly, the fact is being exploited by politicians from motives of 'public expediency'. These are the words of Mr Asquith who, with Mr Lloyd George, made rather sentimental references to the war work of women. Precious time is being wasted upon the Electoral Reform Bill which, in giving votes to women householders over 30, quite excludes female munitions workers, the very class the measure is supposed to favour.

> *The country has never been consulted on this matter anyhow, and it seems the height of political profligacy to rush this thing through at this time. Nobody predicts that it will bring any benefits, and the fairest course would be to take a referendum of the whole people on this question as soon as possible after the war, when the matter could be judged from the new outlook, and with the new knowledge.[23]*

Another item, headed 'Patriotism at a price', subjected the readers of one paper in 1916 to what appeared to be an extended and vitriolic editorial attack on female suffrage. What follows is just a part of it:

> *Innumerable speeches have been made and articles written, claiming that women's war work entitles them to the Parliamentary franchise. No organised political party in the country, other than the suffragists, thus takes advantage of the nation's needs to further its own ends. Incidentally they arrogate to themselves the right to speak for all women, ignoring the fact that many thousands of women, themselves engaged in the most important national and charitable work repudiate the claim of the suffragists to voice their opinions.*
>
> *The Parliamentary vote is not something to be bartered away for any 'services rendered'. It is not a right, but a duty and a responsibility . . . If the vote were merely an order of merit it would have been due to and conferred upon women before now; women have not served the state for the first time during this war . . . the state already discriminates between its male citizens, many of whom have no vote, and do not clamour for one, though they are performing the noblest and most heroic service in this great struggle. Nothing can be more illogical than to claim that because women can serve the state nobly and effectively in their own way, therefore they have the right to govern it. There is no question of abandoning constitutional government in favour of a military despotism on account of the heroic deeds of our army. Why then should there be any talk of feminine government because women have shown themselves ready to serve the country in its need?*
>
> *The fact is however that the claim of Votes for Women as a reward for war work is altogether unsound. Close up our ranks and get on with the war.[24]*

Only when the reader got to the very end of the piece did they learn that it was a paid-for advertisement by the Woking Branch of something called the National League for Opposing Women Suffrage, and that the paper's editor disassociated himself from the views expressed. Another body – the Women's International League – were anxious to impress upon new women voters the responsibilities attached to the franchise, which in their view extended to becoming an expert on foreign policy:

> *Women should remember two maxims: 'the price of liberty is eternal vigilance' and 'knowledge will always trample upon ignorance'. The latter must especially be taken to heart concerning international affairs. We saw this War break upon us unprepared. We, men as well as women, had neglected to keep ourselves informed on matters of foreign policy. The Germans may have made this war inevitable at the moment, but we also are responsible – men more than women*

since they had political power, but women too, a little. Therefore the Women's International League appeals to women to grapple with this immensely difficult job of foreign policy.[25]

Dedicated followers of fashion

But never mind the war effort! Never mind the franchise! *Coming Fashions* magazine was still able to rise serenely above the carnage of war in 1915, to lay down the minutely detailed dictates of the coming season's fashion, as this extract, reported in the *Berkshire Chronicle*, shows:

> Shot silks and flowered gauzes, embroidered muslins and old world prints and cottons will be quite in keeping with the sloping shoulders and the flounced skirts . . . that we shall walk in silk attire at all hours of the day this summer is now a foregone conclusion.[26]

Come the summer sales and the talk was all of economy (not least to release funds for investment in War Bonds). Fashion salesladies were asked how their customers should practise economy, and their answers were both predictable and off-the-wall:

SALE
of
High Class
Models....

OWEN
OWEN LTD

will offer on
MONDAY NEXT
and throughout the week,

BEAUTIFUL .....
COSTUMES, GOWNS,
COATS, BLOUSES,
LACES, TRIMMINGS,
UNDERWEAR, SILKS ETC
together with a Very Large
Assortment of
"PESCO"
UNDERWEAR
also hundreds of dozens of rich quality
KID & SUEDE GLOVES
At Remarkably Low Prices.
SEE WINDOWS.
Catalogues Free By Post.
POST ORDERS MUCH ESTEEMED.
Owen Owen Ltd, LONDON ROAD
LIVERPOOL.

> The way to accommodate in dress is to take advantage of the low prices, which are a rather unexpected feature of the summer sales this year, and to lay in as much stock as possible for the future. No one in our business can predict what the future may bring . . . and my advice to every woman is to double her purchases now, and be on the right side.[27]

Even in the middle of the war, there appeared to be none of the shortages and austerity that characterised the 1939–45 conflict:

> Winter sales are now in full swing and many folk will welcome them with joy. This year the bargains are more wonderful than ever

Little sign of wartime austerity for this ladies' outfitter.

and it is quite possible to buy a smart street coat or a pretty frock for half the price asked for it two months ago.[28]

By 1917, the retailers had a further sales incentive at their disposal – the threat of future shortages posed by the moves towards a total war economy:

The January Sales

In pre-war days, that now seem so distant, the first of January was one of the red-letter days of the year, for the feminine members of the family. On that date the drapers and milliners were wont to hold high festival, and to make their first yearly so-called sacrifice of choice wares. The war

Shopping becomes part of the war effort.

had mostly put an end to the sales, although not perhaps to the sacrifices, to judge from shop windows and catalogues, and in many directions prices are low enough to tempt buyers, even in wartime. The drapers and tailors however sound a note of warning, and point out that as the year advances everything will be much dearer, and more difficult to procure since there will be in the near future further withdrawals of skilled workers from industrial centres, and common everyday articles used by all classes will be hard to come by . . . but the patriotic woman will buy only what is indispensable to her comfort and wellbeing.[29]

By now there were even hints of wartime austerity casting its shadow over ladies' fashion:

In these terrible war days we have no use for the smart garden party gowns and evening frocks, in which we used to make so brave a show . . . everything is very simple this year. Simplicity of cut and of trimming characterises all the models, and anything elaborate is out of place. Some say, no doubt, we shall go back to our feathers and furbelows – but not at present.[30]

Some clothing retailers at least had their eye firmly on the demands of war. Hedgecocks advertised themselves as the Reading Mourning Warehouse, specialising in meeting the needs of the bereaved and promising to give their orders top priority. However, they may have found their core business threatened, as did this dressmaker in Portsmouth:

This war has sadly interfered with our employment, especially in Portsmouth. In

*several papers it has recently been suggested by leading ladies of Society that, as
an emblem of mourning a badge is all that needs to be worn. Now, sir, this must
more than ever interfere with our trade.*[31]

But the clothing industry would not be out of work if all fashion-conscious young widows
followed the minute dictates of this column (the following extract only takes us from the
neck upwards):

*The young widow generally chooses a small hat of black corded silk with a long
veil of cotton and falling in rich sort folds down the back, the effect being very
becoming to the face . . . Jet ornaments are worn during the first month, but
afterwards many young widows wear their pearls.*[32]

By 1917 the growing independence of women war workers was starting to lead to a
revolution in their mode of dress:

*Some of the munitions girls have taken to wearing trousers, and appear proud of
them. It is not so startling an innovation as would have shocked old-fashioned
people only a few years ago. The land girls have for some time donned breeches
and gaiters, an attire which looks very business-like, while others engaged in
occupations hitherto restricted to men, have more or less favoured masculine
garments. The police look on with wondering, possibly also admiring, eyes
recollecting that it would have been their duty not long since to arrest such for
masquerading in masculine attire. But many changes have happened under the
rule of DORA. The point seems rather obscure whether men can if they choose
adopt feminine apparel. But there does not appear any great desire. But trousers
have ceased to be the distinguishing garb of the sexes.*[33]

Not everybody was delighted by this change in ladies' fashion. Four munitions girls who
refused to wear trousers at work found themselves sacked and their appeal against
dismissal refused. The call for more women to work outdoors on the land had an
additional hazard for the fashion-conscious:

*One of the disadvantages of the low-necked blouses now so freely worn is that
the skin is apt to become tanned owing to exposure to wind and sun. In some
cases the exposure causes a red tinge, which becomes unsightly when one
changes into a decollete evening frock.*[34]

The article went on to offer a detailed regime, involving a good toilet cream, white
powder and a vigorous rub down with a chamois leather, so the disfigurement will never
occur. Where necks did get burned, they recommended treatment with hydrogen peroxide
(a chemical also used for hair bleach, limescale removal and, in the next war, to power
Hitler's V2 rockets).

Finally, in another acknowledgement of wartime conditions, the fashion-conscious
woman was told how to dress in the blackout:

*The darkness of the streets in wartime has led to many suggestions for the benefit
of pedestrians who are in danger of colliding with each other, and to not a few
inventions with a similar object. Women have been advised to wear white hats at*

night, but these are only visible for a short distance; luminous buttons were then invented, and after a trial were found to fit the need. These have been followed by luminous collars, for which a patent has lately been applied by the inventors, who claim great things for their device, which glows with great brilliance, and the darker the night, the greater the light emitted. The collars should be worn throughout the day in order that they may absorb the light; they are made of the best materials, in all the fashionable shapes, and are very dainty and pretty. The luminosity lasts for years; no poisonous chemicals are used in their preparation, nor are the collars inflammable . . . feathers, birds and other decorations for hats have also been rendered luminous by means of radium and phosphorus.[35]

So much for blackout precautions! All the Zeppelins had to do was to look out for all those women, glowing in the dark!

Chapter 7
Learning to Hate the Hun

To Germinate is to become a naturalised German

Schoolboy howler © 1915

Before the war, the British public had been fed a series of best-selling novels alerting them to the dangers of German spies – such as Erskine Childers' *The Riddle of the Sands* (1903), William Le Queux's *The Invasion of 1910* (1906) and *Spies of the Kaiser* (1909), and Saki's *When William Came* (1914). In the real world, British counter-intelligence, or MO5, was active in looking for possible espionage agents well before the formal outbreak of war. In particular, they became suspicious of a barber's shop in the Caledonian Road, run by one Karl Gustav Ernst, the son of a German émigré. They obtained permission to intercept his mail, which revealed a network of twenty-two paid spies, based in strategic locations such as Chatham and Portland. They were all rounded up on the day war broke out. The following day a further 21 confirmed and some 200 suspected German agents were taken into custody under the new Aliens Restrictions Order. At a stroke, German espionage suffered a blow from which it would never properly recover for the duration of the war.

Ernst's case got to trial in November and he was sentenced to seven years, but he might be considered to have got off lightly. Under the Defence of the Realm Act (DORA), espionage became a military offence, potentially punishable by death. The death sentence was indeed meted out to a number of agents who tried to slip into the country after the declaration of war. One of these, Carl Lody, became in November 1914 the first man in 150 years to be executed at the Tower of London. Lody was a German naval reserve lieutenant, who arrived in the country posing as an American tourist. He was ill-trained and was quickly picked up by counter-intelligence. Although his amateurish activities posed little real threat to Britain, his trial – which the authorities allowed to be covered by the press – did a lot to fuel spy mania among the population at large. A further ten German agents met similar fates at the Tower.

The Aliens Restriction Order imposed some quite strict limits on aliens and stiff penalties for breaching them. There were restrictions on them owning such things as firearms, motor vehicles, petrol, homing pigeons and radio equipment. They had to register with the authorities and were barred from certain restricted areas (principally coastal and military districts) and from the banking industry. Members of the Stock Exchange were required to identify any enemy aliens in their employ. In a number of British towns and cities all German males of military age were rounded up within days of war starting. One Hans von Chorus (incidentally, the son of a German general) earned himself six months' imprisonment for possessing a motorcycle without the permission of the Chief Constable, and Marie Ann Schmidt was fined £5 (or three months' imprisonment) for travelling more than 5 miles from her registered address without a permit. Some breaches appeared to be relatively innocent. Mary Warni had lived in England for twenty years. She led a relatively sheltered (not to say housebound) life, caring for her elderly parents and had been advised by someone that it was not necessary for German women to register as aliens. The authorities took a relatively lenient line with her, fining her just £1.

The regulations governing the registration of aliens illustrated one of the ways in which married women were still the chattels of their husbands:

A married woman is of the same nationality as her husband even after his death and widows who have been married to Germans should put themselves right under the new regulations dealing with aliens. A British- or Irish-born woman may obtain a certificate of readmission to British nationality without taking out naturalisation papers, which cost £3.[1]

Spy fever

But the arrests and restrictions did not stop a wave of sometimes hysterical spy fever sweeping the country when war broke out, with the most innocent of actions being interpreted as espionage. If one believed all the rumours, the Germans had already invaded in numbers. One had apparently been caught inside the waterworks at Aldershot with a quantity of poison about his person. Dozens of others had been planted inside the utility companies, ready to wreak havoc when the prospect of invasion drew near. Our essential infrastructure had already been attacked and damaged in key locations, and the nocturnal coastline must have been virtually as bright as day, from all the agents reported to be shining signal lights to German submarines. A sensationalist book *German Spies in London*, sold 40,000 copies in the first week after its publication in 1915.

The hysteria of the day also gave rise to that perennial favourite, the German spy disguised as a nun. The *Liverpool Post* reported a Merseyside lady travelling to London in the ladies-only compartment of a train and finding herself sitting opposite two nuns with suspiciously masculine wrists. She reported the matter to the guard and the two dangerous spies were detained on their arrival. Or so the story goes.

Suspicious events were attributed to enemy aliens on the slightest of evidence or, as in this case, apparently none at all.

A warehouse at the Ship Canal Docks, Salford has to be added to the list of mysterious cotton fires which have taken place in this district of late. Here as in the other cases there is reasonable ground for suspicion that it is an act of incendiarism by the enemy in our midst.[2]

Despite offering no grounds for this assertion, the paper went on to campaign for the introduction of 'fire inquests'.

Rumours abounded that German-born grocers were slowly poisoning our food, while a German barber was just as likely to cut your throat as your hair. German foodstuffs themselves became objects of suspicion; one grocer changed the name of German sausage to Empire sausage and referred to it as 'good British viands'. Elsewhere, sauerkraut was re-branded liberty cabbage and wieners became hot dogs. On the subject of dogs, dachshunds were kicked and abused in the street (though German shepherd dogs were instead re-branded Alsatians, and thus were held to come from a disputed part of France, rather than Germany; this was perhaps a pragmatic move, in that an Alsatian was rather better placed than a dachshund to retaliate if kicked).

Even the Mayor of Deal was arrested on suspicion of espionage, as was one of the clergymen ministering to the troops based on the Isle of Wight. In May 1915, the Revd I. Switer, who had been transferred from his church to the Isle of Wight, was passing his off-duty hours walking the coast at Freshwater. He had with him some binoculars, and he made the mistake of looking seawards, just as some ships happened to be passing. He was promptly arrested by some soldiers and taken, blindfolded, to their fort. Only after somebody recognised him did they release him. Elsewhere, an artist (apparently well-known, though un-named by the newspaper) set up his easel on a riverbank to capture an attractive scene of a rustic bridge across the waterway, and was promptly arrested by the Army as a spy who was gathering information about this vital part of Britain's defences.

Elsewhere, caches of weapons were found. Some thought they were the property of spy rings, though wiser heads decided they had probably been dumped by those in fear of prosecution under DORA. Extra guards were placed on military establishments and the authorities on the Isle of Wight warned the public not to approach them at night, for fear of being shot. It is not clear whether similar warnings were issued at Edinburgh and Birkenhead, but two soldiers were said to have been shot while approaching military establishments there. The words 'said to have been' are used advisedly, since an alternative conspiracy theory has it that these shootings were invented, so as to keep all concerned on their toes. There were, however, confirmed cases of civilians being shot by over-zealous (or nervous) sentries.

Even the humble pigeon became an object of suspicion, as the *Racing Pigeon* magazine confirmed:

> *The Germans have for years been training racing pigeons to fly from England.*
> *Their government subsidises lofts of pigeons, which are kept in various places,*
> *including the forts. These pigeons have no doubt been used by spies for many*
> *years.*[3]

German trawlers captured in the North Sea were said to have baskets of message-carrying pigeons with a range of more than 1,000 miles. The most chance association with pigeons could land you in trouble. One alien was sentenced to six months' imprisonment, on no stronger evidence than the word of a former Army officer's wife, that:

> *On Tuesday afternoon, I was on Primrose Hill when the prisoner passed by, and*
> *I noticed a pigeon on a level with his head, and about three yards in front of him,*
> *flying away with a little white paper under its wing.*[4]

Another innocent party had a hostile crowd assemble outside his house when somebody else's pigeon stopped for a rest on his roof. Any premises occupied by enemy nationals were automatically suspect. Their tennis courts, flat roofs or paved gardens became, in the public imagination, gun platforms for use in shelling nearby strategic targets, in the event of an invasion.

Nor was the obsession with spies confined to the general public. Winston Churchill was seized by it and, on one occasion, led a rather drunken raiding party on a nearby house from where, it was reported, someone had been signalling out to sea. The owner, former Conservative MP Arthur Bignold, was held at gunpoint while the property was searched.

The BBC was still almost a decade away when war was declared, but the potential of radio as a means of transmitting information was well understood. A popular play, *The Man who Stayed at Home*, did much to perpetuate fears about its use in espionage. Professor Arthur Schuster had been German-born but educated in England. He had risen to become a leading British academic, and the brother of a senior figure in the banking industry. When he was discovered to have a wireless receiver in his house, along with 'a quantity of insulated and ordinary wire', dark rumours began to circulate about espionage. The authorities impounded it, but it was established: (a) that the apparatus could not transmit, only receive, messages; (b) that it was not sensitive enough to pick up broadcasts from Germany; and (c) that Professor Schuster had only used it to pick up time signals from the transmitter on the Eiffel Tower. Any suggestion that it had been used for 'traitorous purposes' was, we were assured, 'a gross and cruel libel'.

This is not to say that there was no genuinely suspicious behaviour going on. Johannes Ramm claimed to be an unemployed book-keeper, who had only been in England for three months. Police investigations revealed that he had in fact been in the country for three years, during which time he had made seven return visits to Germany. He was suspiciously well off for someone who had never worked during his time in England, showed an unhealthy interest in local troop movements and had been trying to communicate with Germany via a neutral country. His fate was placed in the hands of the military authorities.

Another German, Johann Lotzsch, passed himself off as Swiss and secured a job with a toy factory. Police investigations identified his true nationality and he initially told them that he had been ineligible for the German Army, on account of being too short. Further enquiries revealed that he was actually a member of the German Army reserve, which meant that the most charitable interpretation had to be that he was in England as a draft dodger. Meanwhile, at the Admiralty wireless station at Waltham near Grimsby two men were seen acting suspiciously. After a chase, one of them was detained. It was thought that they were looking for the power supply to the station, no doubt with a view to cutting it.

Hating the Hun

This was the first real propaganda war. In a modern society, almost everyone – civilian or enlisted – has to be to some degree committed to the war effort. To maintain this, the authorities need to create a consensus that theirs is a just war and the other side the barbaric aggressors.

The same propaganda also has an international application, in getting non-aligned countries more sympathetic to your cause and, ideally, siding with you against the enemy.

The Germans were rather quicker off the mark with this than the British. Before the outbreak of the Great War, they set up their Central Office for Foreign Services, whose job was to distribute German propaganda abroad. They also used mobile cinemas to take propaganda to front-line German troops, either to maintain morale or to get them fighting mad. In Britain, responsibility for propaganda fell initially to a branch of military intelligence, MI5(h) which, from 16 January 1917, became MI7.

The Germans gave Britain no shortage of material with which to demonise them. Leaving aside all the stories of individual atrocities, they conducted air raids on civilian populations, introduced poison gas and flame throwers as weapons of war and introduced submarine warfare against merchant shipping. On 17 May 1915, the Cunard liner *Lusitania* was torpedoed by a German submarine within sight of the Irish coast. It sank within 20 minutes, with the loss of 1,198 people, 124 of them American citizens. The sinking prompted outrage on both sides of the Atlantic, and led to further attacks on foreign aliens and their property. On the Western Front, some of the Allied troops took to shouting 'Remember the Lusitania, you murderous swine!' as they charged the enemy trenches. It all added weight to the British portrayal of the Germans as unprincipled savages.

The Home Secretary felt compelled to respond to the wave of anti-German feeling that accompanied the outbreak of war:

> *The public can rest assured that the great majority of Germans remaining in this country are peaceful and innocent persons from whom no danger is to be feared.*[5]

Others – but only a few others – also pleaded in the local press for tolerance:

> *May I make an appeal to the sense of fair play and justice of my fellow townspeople on behalf of innocent Germans and people with German-sounding names now living in and around Newbury. I am sure that anyone would deplore anything of an unfriendly gesture by act or word towards them. If our own people, in a foreign land, have been insulted, that is no reason why any innocent law-abiding German should have such treatment at the hands of the English . . .*[6]

> *We do not hold the comforting fiction that German spies are creations of the imagination, nor do we deny the possible menace of the large number of Germans in our midst. But it is patent that there are thousands of inoffensive Germans here, who deserve, as they are generally receiving, every consideration at our hands. The likeness between ourselves and the German people has probably been over-estimated . . . It is with the Latin races that Englishmen in general have the greater affinity . . . [as for the*

A journey the *Lusitania* would never make, for it was torpedoed and sunk on the inbound journey to Liverpool on 7 May 1915.

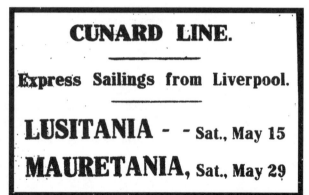

CUNARD LINE.

Express Sailings from Liverpool.

LUSITANIA - - Sat., May 15

MAURETANIA, Sat., May 29

Allied public opinion was outraged by the sinking of the *Lusitania*. Among those killed were 124 American citizens, bringing America closer to declaring war.

German . . . We respect him. To love him is perhaps rather difficult. But at least we can treat him well.[7]

It did no good. *The Times* probably summed up the mood of the British nation in 1914:

Many of the Germans still in London are unquestionably agents of the German government, however loose the tie may be . . . They had in their possession arms, wireless telegraph apparatus, aeroplane equipment, motor cars, carrier pigeons and other material that might be useful to the belligerent. The weapons seized by the police make an extensive armoury . . .

It has been remarked by the observant that German tradesmen's shops are frequently to be found in close proximity to vulnerable points in the chain of London's communications such as railway bridges . . .

The German barber seems to have little time for sabotage. He is chiefly engaged in removing the 'Kaiser' moustaches of his compatriots. They cannot, however, part with the evidences of their nationality altogether, for the tell-tale hair of the Teuton will show the world that new Smith is but old Schmidt writ small.[8]

Since the sinking of the Lusitania *a new spirit has come over the British nation the world over. The regrettable anti-German incidents are but a manifestation of the outraged feelings of the people – of their detestation of the brutal German nation that is guilty of such unspeakable atrocities as the murder of women and children . . . But while these demonstrations are evidence of the growth of anti-German feeling it would be a mistake to allow violence towards the aliens in this country. It is for the government to take action and place these people in a place of safety for themselves and where they can do no harm to the country.[9]*

From early in 1915, a public debate began as to how we should treat the Germans, once they had been defeated. Dr Lyttelton, the Headmaster of Eton College, made the mistake of suggesting in public that we should not humiliate them. This outraged the editor of the local paper, who described it as namby-pamby misguided sentimentality:

leniency of treatment would be absolutely lost upon the Germans. They would regard it as another sign of weakness, and as proof of the recognition of the superiority of the German.

Far from being saved from their own vindictiveness the Germans badly want a lesson. They not only want to taste the bitterness and humiliation of defeat. They want to know what it is to have the ravages of war in their own country . . . For all the damage and spoliation they must be made to pay. France must have back her lost provinces, and there will have to be a rectification of the eastern frontier.[10]

All in all, it should come as no surprise that hatred of the Hun became focussed in an Anti-German Union. In June 1915 an announcement appeared in the small advertisements section of the local papers:

The Anti-German Union
No German labour
No German goods
No German influence
Britain for the British
Aims of the Union:

(1)   To foster national ideals and to keep alive the patriotic spirit of the people;
(2)   To defend British freedom, rights and privileges from German invasion;

(3)   To defend British industry and British labour against German competition;

(4)   To fight against German influences in our social and financial, and industrial and political life.

Readers were invited to send off for membership forms and details of how these objectives were to be achieved. One paper thought it was an excellent idea:

Germans not only infest this country, as they do other countries, to spy, but there is ample evidence from Belgium, France and other countries that they are there to give these countries a stab in the back at an opportune time. It is also fairly well-established that practically all over the world German gold has been and is being used in endeavours to suborn the press and secure publication of German views. Further, we know every effort has been made to place Germans of influence in high places, and in our own country they have not merely made their way into high financial positions but they have reached the Privy Council. We do not say that every German is a black sheep, but the evidence is overwhelming that a large proportion are merely serving the German government in the countries of their adoption and are not particular as to the means of doing so.[11]

In addition to being anti-German, the Union (which became the British Empire Union from 1916) was also anti-socialist (they believed the Labour Party would 'Bolshevise Britain' and wanted a paramilitary force to be established to prevent this) and had links with anti-semitic groups, though those aspects of its policy were not clear from the following manifesto:

This Union has been formed to unite British-born men and women without respect to party, class or creed in order to foster national ideals and to keep alive the patriotic spirit of the people; to defend British freedom, rights and privileges against German aggression and British labour against German competition; and to fight against German influence in our social, financial, political and industrial life. In an explanation of aim and policy, the founders remark that Germans still hold positions of trust in Government departments, in Parliament and on the Privy Council; Germans, instead of Britons, are executing many Government contracts. Thousands of enemy aliens are still at large even in prohibited areas; cotton for explosives still reached the enemy and is not yet even declared contraband; Germans still dominate our financial and business houses; Germans trade under English names. Mysterious fires and explosions still occur in our docklands, manufactories and warships. The Union proposes by issuing publications, by holding meetings, by the personal efforts of members and through the Public Press to strengthen the hands of the Government to deal with these evils.[12]

The anger of the British public was not limited to kicking small dogs. German-owned shops and restaurants were attacked and looted, and the proprietors of many such businesses suddenly discovered that they in fact had Swiss or some other neutral ancestry. A mob estimated at 5,000 roamed the streets of Chatham, attacking anything remotely Germanic. As a consequence, 200 police and 350 soldiers were needed to restore order.

The Riot Act had to be read in Peterborough. Elsewhere, bands of vigilantes were formed, which were only eventually brought under some form of official control by the formation of the Volunteer Training Corps, a forerunner of the Home Guard.

Some Germans were war-mongers, but in a surprising way. A 1915 new year's message from a Socialist body, the German Humanity League, called upon non-aligned countries to take up arms, but for the other side:

> *We appeal to our brethren on the Continent of Europe and in the United States not to hide themselves behind the screen of neutrality. We are face to face with the enemies of mankind. The German nation, driven into a wicked war by the Kaiser and his military 'entourage', cajoled by perjured statesmen in the Reichstag and by false records circulated in every state in order to deceive our compatriates, has recklessly hurled itself blindfold against forces which, sustained by indisputable moral considerations, show no signs of weakening in their determination to expel from Belgium the troops which have covered her habitations with blood and irreparably injured an innocent nation our rulers had sworn to protect. We ask you to remember that the territory of no German state has been menaced by the allies, who are lawfully and honourably defending the plain rights of the cruelly outraged Belgians.[13]*

The Aliens' response

Small wonder, in the light of so much hostility, that enemy aliens went on the defensive. One German-born resident of Worthing not only failed to register as an alien, but also dyed his black hair auburn and barricaded himself inside his house. The most tenuous connection with Germany could leave you open to suspicion (or the victim of paranoia). Mr E.F.M. Sutton was Manchester born and bred, resident there since 1867, but had felt it necessary to change his name from Sussman at the outbreak of war. His father had been a Danish citizen, who had lived in Schleswig-Holstein prior to its annexation by Germany in 1864, but had been a British citizen for forty years. Despite what appear to be impeccable nationality credentials, Mr Sutton still found it incumbent on himself to resign his public office, as a member of Manchester's Prison Visiting Committee, in 1917.

But it was not just paranoia on Mr Sutton's part. Even British birth and British citizenship could still leave you under suspicion:

> *Notices to quit the area were on Tuesday served by the police on behalf of the military authorities on persons regarded as undesirable residents in coastal towns adjoining the Tyneside District. The people affected included alien enemies and naturalised citizens of both sexes, also British-born descendents of aliens, including even the second generation. Exemptions have been made in cases of advanced age and extreme youth.[14]*

In fact, some correspondents thought the naturalised aliens were the worst, for:

> *The most dangerous of alien enemies were to be found among those who had become naturalised, and were thus in a position to pose as friends . . . Undoubtedly all Germans and Austrians in our midst should be placed behind*

barbed wire, and, if they happen to have English wives, these should be interned with their husbands.[15]

As in the Second World War, precious little real evidence of spies came to light, and a number of those registered as enemy aliens asked to be naturalised as English. The rush to secure British citizenship was such that the legal stationers ran out of the necessary application forms. Some already had been naturalised, but still felt it necessary to advertise the fact:

Dear Sir,

Will you allow me through the medium of your paper to inform my numerous patrons and the public generally, that I am a naturalised Englishman, having lived in this country for thirty-four years and having taken the oath of allegiance over two years ago . . . I am proud to know that I am a naturalised Englishman.

Yours faithfully,

F.H.R. Scheibner[16]

Some non-aliens got caught up in the witch-hunt simply on account of their names. Leaving aside for a moment the Royal Family (the house of Saxe-Coburg became Windsor during the conflict), Mr Basil Hinderberg was the British-born conductor of an orchestra, who decided in the face of public opinion to change his name to Cameron. The Kleiser Brothers, jewellers and watchmakers, found it necessary to publish a disclaimer to rumours that they had been detained as enemy aliens. They, too, were British born and bred. Count Falkenstein was also found guilty in the court of public opinion of being suspiciously foreign-sounding, and was reported as being Austrian. Police duly raided his house and seized some of his property, only to discover that he was in fact Swedish. The shame-faced officers apologised and returned his goods.

Some Aliens were (illegally) equipped to defend themselves. One Franz Hecht was arrested for having a revolver which he said he carried for his own protection, but the court records suggest he may have been his own worst enemy when it came to courting trouble, for:

He had boasted that he was as good as four Englishmen, and several people had threatened to throw him into the river.[17]

He was fined £2. Even more provocative was revolver-toting Thomas Selle of Woking. He had been heard boasting drunkenly about possessing homing pigeons and being in touch with his native Germany. When the authorities came to visit him they found the revolver, but any pigeons had flown the coop. His boasts cost him a substantial £50 fine. But Austrian Emile Medinger had enough weaponry to equip a small army. Visiting police found a total of twelve firearms and a substantial quantity of ammunition. This cost Mr Medinger a £100 fine.

Some German-born residents sought to answer their native country's call and return home to join the German Army. For some eighty-five would-be German soldiers that journey was a short one; they were arrested and taken prisoners of war while awaiting a boat to carry them to the Continent. They were paraded through the streets and booed by the public, who took them to be spies until disabused. Most of the Germans were said to be 'delighted with their fate'.

Many German expatriates found themselves dismissed from their jobs when war broke out. Reports came in of large numbers of German reservists, discharged from the British vessels they crewed, wandering around Cardiff, destitute. In Liverpool, there were an estimated 1,500 foreigners stranded, many of them needing charitable aid. A meeting was called at the Town Hall, with the intention of setting up an International Relief Committee, but this received a very dusty response from many of those attending. They said that if the aliens needed help, their governments could send it via the (then neutral) American Consul. Their position was contrasted with the treatment reported to have been meted out to the Belgians, during the invasion of their country.

Prisoners of war

The war led to one massive influx of German men into the country – as prisoners of war. By November 1914, just one German prisoner-of-war camp, at Newbury Race Course, already held some 3,000 inmates. It was visited by the Prime Minister, Herbert Asquith and his wife and, according to British press reports, many of the inmates cheered them. According to one of their guards:

Some of them are jolly well pleased to be where they are. They are treated very well here, have good food, comfortable tents to sleep in, and perfect liberty, except that they are not allowed out of the compound. They are very quiet, except at night and then they make a frightful row with their singing and shouting.[18]

The German press was telling a very different story. Referring to 'the Newbury Scandal', they claimed that the prisoners were being kept thirty to a 'stall' (whatever one of those was), made to sleep on damp bare earth and starved. It was claimed that two inmates had died as a result, and that German women were also being interned. Officials from the American State Department were brought in to investigate these claims independently, but they could find no basis for them. The commandant was found to be 'on the best of terms with his prisoners'.

An Austrian former prisoner of war at the Newbury Camp totally rebutted German stories of atrocities:

I most emphatically deny the occurrence of any ill-treatment or atrocities at any time at Newbury. Anyone making such accusations is telling deliberate falsehoods.[19]

He went on to describe the system of self-government that operated at the camp, with regular inspections by the camp commandant and a well-established (if rarely needed) complaints procedure. All inmates had the right to address the commandant directly, as he made his daily round.

At another camp, at Frimley in Surrey, the complaints were not about the guards, but about the general public. Some 5,000 prisoners were being held there by the end of September 1914 and they were starting to feel more like zoological exhibits.

Hordes of people gathered at the railway station to witness their arrival, but the curiosity did not end there. There was a solid stream of sightseers going to and from the camp the next weekend, with some of them taking photographs through the wire and even a moving picture producer filming them. The German propaganda machine picked up on this and presented it as mistreatment. One correspondent, at least, called for this to stop:

> *Surely we want the prisoners to go back with such a kindly recollection of their treatment as shall help towards a better state of feeling between us in days to come.*[20]

But any kindly recollections they took home would not be enough to ward off a repeat of the unpleasantness in 1939.

Chapter 8

The War Effort

*Make use of your motor car for Red Cross purposes. Have the present motor
body removed and an ambulance body fitted in its place by Gandy and Sons.*

Advertisement in the *Hampshire Chronicle*
2 January 1915

*Buy advertised goods in wartime. Because while other things are dearer, the
prices of advertised articles remain the same.*

An advertisement for advertising – *Liverpool Courier*
1915

Paying for the war

War on the scale at which it was being waged required huge amounts of funding. Overall
government expenditure, which had stood at £192 millions in 1913, rose to
£2,579 millions by 1918. Only about a third of this was paid for by taxation; the rest was
added to the national debt, through borrowing. War Bonds, sold to patriotic members of
the public, were an important part of this fund-raising. As in the Second World War,
communities set themselves some ambitious targets. In Reading, Business Man's Week
was launched in 1918 by the Chamber of Commerce with the object of raising £250,000
– enough to provide the Royal Navy with a monitor (a ship to help tackle the submarine
menace). One of the best ways to get citizens to put their hands in their pockets was to
put on a display of the latest secret weapon:

> *The tank is coming! Newbury is to have its War Bonds Week, and the latest
> engine of warfare is to be the leading feature in the campaign. It will take its
> stand in the Market Place next Thursday and on the following Saturday, and will
> furnish the platform for local orators to make appeals to Newbury people. There
> will be no lack of listeners, for the tank is certain to attract a big crowd both of
> town and country residents.[1]*

This tank was the very latest model (less favoured communities got war-battered second-
hand ones). It was on its way to France and, in consequence, no member of the public
was allowed to peek inside or even to ask questions about it. The crew were, in any event,
under strict orders to disavow all knowledge of its workings (implausibly, given that they
drove it there and took it off to an undisclosed destination at the end of fund-raising).

The wounded

Never in history has better or more skilful attention been given to the wounded than during the present great war, and the petrol-driven motor ambulance and hospital have given invaluable aid in the great work of mercy. Throughout the war-swept area red-cross conveyances of the allied forces are run upon

'SHELL'
MOTOR SPIRIT

and can therefore be thoroughly depended upon. It is well to remember when purchasing petrol to say 'Shell' and insist upon it. It is supplied for all the services of the allied forces only and is obtainable everywhere.

What the public were told was that they should not draw unkind comparisons between the vehicles and prehistoric animals, or other un-lovable creatures, since the operators 'have developed an affection for these unwieldy monsters, and are disturbed when they are dubbed as giant toads'.

The tank certainly had the required effect on the citizens of Newbury. The appeal raised £120,567, more than twice what was itself thought to be an ambitious target. The National War Savings Committee even went so far as to name and shame (or praise) counties, according to how much they raised. In March 1918, Northumberland (14*s* and 5*d* per head of population) and Warwickshire (14/2) headed the league table of war savers, while Cornwall (1/7) and Cheshire (2/2) came bottom.

But, in order to buy War Bonds, the public had first to make economies elsewhere. As ever, there was no shortage of advice as to how this might be done – though not all of it may have been of great help to the average man in the street:

Many people are asking, in view of the campaign of retrenchment 'How can I save?' The Parliamentary War Savings Committee are at no loss for suggestions on this point:

Their idea of austerity included the following:

No one should build a house for himself at this time. Moving (unless to a cheaper house) should be avoided . . .

The wealthy landowner with more than one estate should reduce his establishments as far as practicable, and the business or professional man with a town house or a country cottage should consider whether he could not dispense with the cottage . . .

The expenditure on flower gardens should be reduced, and as much of the garden as

Brito margarine, temporarily unobtainable, patriotically gives its advertising space over to the National War Bonds campaign.

The B*r*ito Buys' War Appeals:

It is your duty to

BUY

NATIONAL

WAR BONDS

They are an insurance of everything you most value—your country—your home—your family—your savings— your very liberty.

This space is given in aid of the Government's appeal to the Nation—in place of the usual advertising on behalf of—

BRITO MARGARINE

temporarily unobtainable. As soon as supplies and cost of manufacture enable it to be produced at the Controller's price, viz., 1/4 a pound, this most delicious of all Margarines will reappear on everybody's breakfast table.

THE ENGLISH MARGARINE WORKS LTD., BROAD GREEN.

possible should be used for growing vegetables . . .

The staff of servants should be reduced wherever possible, and, in particular, male servants should not be employed . . .

A saving that could be made is in the abandonment or greatly reduced consumption of wine, beer and spirits. The custom of 'treating' should be given up as a fruitful source of unnecessary drinking.

In many establishments more could probably be saved by a return to simpler meals than even by economy in the quality or quantity of the articles consumed. The mere change from a five-course dinner to the old-fashioned two-course meal might enable some families to dispense with one servant, quite apart from other economies . . .

With the stoppage or great reduction on entertaining there should be little or no demand for evening dresses, dress suits, etc. . . .

All not strictly necessary extras, such as veils, white gloves, furs, silk garments, should not be bought.

The expenditure on tennis clubs, golf clubs, rowing clubs, etc. should be strictly limited, as also subscriptions to West End clubs.

Among the well-to-do classes, expenditure on hunting, shooting, horse

HAVE <u>YOU</u> HELPED YOUR COUNTRY?

Thousands of our bravest and best are willing to GIVE their lives for Britain. Is it too much to ask you to LEND your money to help them in their fight for freedom?

<u>YOU</u> CAN BUY WAR BONDS.

racing, etc. should be abandoned, except in so far as the killing of game for food is concerned.[2]

They also pointed out that War Bonds made ideal wedding presents and tips for servants.

Rather more practical advice about war savings came from Sir Robert Blair, London County Council's Education Officer. He pointed out that if every man, woman and child in the country were to save a penny, that would represent £187,500 towards the war effort. And how might those savings be made?

not going to picture palaces, not eating sweets, not riding in trams, buses or trains unnecessarily, being very careful not to waste bread or other kinds of food, taking trouble to learn to cook well so as to make the food taste nice and go further, keeping the cooking pots clean, being careful of your clothes and mending them when they want it, not throwing away any bottles or jam pots, but giving or selling them to people who will use them, being careful of the things at school, like paper and pencils, and even ink.[3]

Others had more radical ideas for savings. The demands of the war effort provided a powerful new argument to those who (in war or peace) wished to see the rates – and public services – cut to the bone. One such wrote to his local paper under the pseudonym 'Taxpayer' in April 1917:

> *It is quite evident that to bring the war to a successful conclusion we must have still more money, and the best way to get it is to economise in the public services. The expenses of the elementary schools should be reduced to the irreducible minimum, the evening schools should be abolished entirely and the cost of administering the National Insurance and Old Age Pensioners Act should be rigidly overhauled (with responsibility for them being handed over to Friendly Societies and the Poor Law Guardians) [the latter the overseers of the Victorian workhouses, then still in operation], . . . There are three new Council schools in Slough and the question is whether they are really necessary under the altered circumstances which have come about.*[4]

His letter encouraged another correspondent, 'Britisher', to float the idea of saving money

Your help is needed!

During the next week the business men of the country, aided by the War Savings Committees, will endeavour to make record sales of National War Bonds and War Savings Certificates. To-day, they ask for your help and support.

In order to achieve the objects of Business Men's Week, each city and town is being asked to buy sufficient National War Bonds and War Savings Certificates to provide the cost of some implement of war. The task allotted to each district is based on an amount of £2 10s. per head of its population.

You are helping your country and yourself when you invest your savings in National War Bonds or War Savings Certificates.

by doing away with free state education altogether (though he recognised this might be a little controversial). Nonetheless:

> *When one sees the lavishness with which they [the Council] spend money on education one wonders whether they have fully yet realised that we are at odds with the most murderous foe that ever faced a nation.[5]*

Another article set out quite a radical statement of the case against compulsory, free state education:

> *What shall we do with our boys? Many a parent will answer this question very simply. 'My boy must look after himself. The state relieves me of all responsibility for his education, which costs me nothing, and except for feeding and clothing him, I do not need to give him a thought for about six or seven years of his life. Then he comes back onto my hands all of a sudden at the age of about thirteen, and I am expected to interest myself in his future and find him something to do. I call it rather hard, and the State might just as well carry on its responsibilities a few more years and see the lad into some occupation.'*

The article acknowledged that these views may not be universal, but argued that they were widely held:

> *And for this reason: As long as a man has to pay for his boy's training, he took some trouble*

*to see he got his money's worth, and the sense of responsibility for the boy was
never entirely absent from his mind. He was, it is true, compelled to send the boy
to school, but the payment of the school pence gave him some choice in the
selection of the school, where there was any choice. Now it all goes by
machinery. It is the old story; you cannot properly value that which costs you
nothing.*[6]

Another novel means of raising funds was floated. Those who thought the idea of
Premium Bonds first saw the light of day in the 1950s should think again. It was proposed
as one way of funding the First World War effort, but received a very dusty reception
from the authorities:

*A very important statement has been made by Sir Robert Kindersley, the
Chairman of the National War Savings Committee, on the question of Premium
Bonds. He sets out plainly that the instinct to save and the instinct to gamble are
not allied but opposed, and any attempt of the state to stimulate the latter will
react unfavourably on the former . . . If once the state gives official approval to
any form of gambling it will sacrifice a main principle. Disguise it as the
advocates may, the Premium Bond is a lottery, and all the specious excuses in the
world will not get rid of this essential defect . . . The appeal of the Premium Bond
is frankly to the baser instinct of cupidity, the desire to 'get-rich-quickly-without-
effort'. It is suggested that the state should deliberately play upon and cultivate
what is well known to be a weakness of human nature – a weakness which has
probably wrought to mankind more mischief in the economic sphere than almost
any other failing.*[7]

War workers and war shirkers

Soldiers at the front did not appreciate the whining (as they saw it) by those back at
home, in reserved occupations, over their conditions of service. Captain Herbert Roberts
took a moment out from being shelled and bombed in his foxhole to offer the local paper
these thoughts on the matter:

*Why does not the Government place the country under martial law? It is drastic,
but these are not the moments for sentimental thoughts; prompt, bold, vigorous
and decisive actions should be the order of the day. Everybody is agreed that the
war must have but one ending – complete success to the Allies. That end will be
gained all the quicker by subordinating every consideration that retards our one
great object, the defeat of a tyrannical, inhuman oppressor.*[8]

One thing guaranteed to raise the blood pressure of serving soldiers was news of men
safely at home going on strike. This man, serving in the Dardanelles, put their views
with particular force:

Dying men curse the strikers

*The only thing that disheartens us is when we get papers and read about the men
striking at home. You have no idea how the men here curse about them; men who
have now gone to their deaths almost cursing their fellow countrymen. I always*

thought I was a very peace-loving chap, but when I read about them I feel absolutely murderous, and wish, as every one of us wishes, that we could be sent home to give them a taste of what we are giving to the Turks. I should feel much more justified in turning a machine gun on those skulking curs than on these Turks, who after all are only doing what they consider is right . . . Do you know what happens to a man that strikes here? He is shot, and that's what should happen to those curs at home.[9]

It was not just serving soldiers who were resentful of the new-found affluence that the war brought to many working people. The Chairman of the Market Bosworth Justices took the opportunity to sound off at two colliers appearing before him:

Some of the working classes . . . are earning more money now than they have ever earned in their lives before, and they would do well to try and save some of it for a rainy day. Times will not always be as they are today. You will be shouting for work in a year or two and you won't find it.[10]

In September 1918 the dispute between members of the forces and those in reserved occupations turned violent. Railwaymen, dissatisfied with an agreement that had been negotiated for them with the management, voted for immediate strike action – and immediate it certainly was. People who had commuted to work by train that morning were left to find their own way back in the evening. Many faced long walks home. A group of wounded ex-servicemen and others, outraged by what they saw as this sabotage of the war effort, stormed the Trade Union Club, the railwaymen's local base. They smashed the windows and door in, threw the furniture about and assaulted and injured a number of policemen who tried to restore order. Some of the wounded soldiers apparently used their crutches as weapons. They then rampaged around the town, and in particular to railway premises. The strikers wisely decided to cancel a planned meeting. There is no doubt where the editor of the local paper's sympathies lay:

The attack on the Trade Union Club in Reading, the headquarters of the local railwaymen, by a number of wounded soldiers is to be deplored, because such exhibitions do more harm than good in the long run. Reason rather than force should guide our actions. But the occurrence is symptomatic of the feeling of those who have been willing to make the supreme sacrifice against the men who stay at home, and who, by striking endanger the lives of the men at the front and hinder the winning of the war . . . The railways are a vital part of the home front, and any cessation of work means the home front is let down. Factories and mines are hindered, munition workers are unable to get to and from their work, and military supplies cannot be carried . . . Moreover the railways are state controlled, and therefore the strike was a strike against the state itself.[11]

Nor was he in any doubt as to where the impetus for the strike came from. The strikers were:

led away by a few Bolsheviks, despite repeated warning against the designs which are at the bottom of Bolshevism and the obvious fact that Bolshevism has ruined Russia.[12]

Some factory employees took their patriotic duties more seriously. Dunlop workers in Birmingham downed tools when rumours began to circulate that their tyres were finding their way to Germany via Denmark. The workers blamed the laxity of the Government, rather than their own management, for this alleged state of affairs, and were only persuaded to return to work following categorical assurances from the Government that this was not actually happening.

TO PATRIOTIC CYCLISTS

whether serving in the Army, as members of Volunteer Defence Corps, or as Special Constables, give your country of your best by fitting

DUNLOP

tyres, which give the minimum of trouble from breakdown, puncture, or skidding. Remember, the better your equipment, the higher your service.

Dunlop appeals for patriotism from the motoring public.

The Liverpool dockers did not even have to go on strike to incur public wrath. The docks were suffering congestion, due to the manpower shortage resulting from recruitment and the high volume of traffic using the port, and an official report blamed the dockers for taking advantage of the situation:

> *The great demand for his services has made him independent; it is only with*
> *difficulty that he can now be induced to work at all, so long as he can find one or*
> *two well-paid jobs to keep him going. The docker will now pick his work, and*
> *any job not offering substantial overtime has no chance with him. He prefers to*
> *start work at midday, work the afternoon shift at the regular rate, and follow on*
> *with overtime at practically double pay.*[13]

The dockers resented this slur on their good name and the next edition carried their detailed rebuttal of the report's conclusions.

Standard of living

The massive investment in the war effort inevitably meant an overall decline in living standards. Consumer expenditure fell by about 20 per cent between 1913 and 1918, not least because the size of the manufacturing workforce supplying civilian needs was reduced to about a third of its pre-war level. However, the nutritional value of the average diet was roughly the same as before the war, and greater efficiency in the manufacturing sector averted any great increase in suffering among the civilian population. After fears at the start of the war that hostilities would lead to mass unemployment, businessmen quickly woke up to the possibility that a successful war might in fact be an opportunity:

> *It was anticipated that the war was going to prove ruinous to the trade and*
> *commerce of the country, but now it appears that out of the great evil may come*
> *much good to British trade. Germany has for long been a most serious*
> *competitor in certain lines of trade and this is the business man's opportunity to*
> *recapture a huge share of this. In foreign trade especially there are now great*

*chances of British manufacturers gaining a footing, for German trading vessels
are held up while British ones may travel almost without hindrance.[14]*

There were claims that some female munitions workers were earning ten times the pay
of an Army corporal facing death in the front line. There were also complaints that some
were spending their new wealth in an immoral and profligate manner (as the debate over
drinking – discussed later – illustrates). But even the supporters of the proletariat had
some rather patronising views on the matter:

*Most artisans' families are in normal times, underfed, inadequately clothed or
otherwise brought up below the health standard. And though the extravagant
way in which wages is spent is to be condemned, yet money is also being spent
on better food for children, warmer underclothes for all members of the family,
more boots and better boots and other things that will make the next generation
stronger and more efficient . . .*

*What is the duty of business men? Surely it is to teach these people how to
spend their money sensibly – how to use it for their own future good and
(incidentally) for the very great advantage of the employing classes, because the
thing most essential to commercial welfare, now and in the future, is a well-fed,
efficient labour supply.[15]*

Our gallant allies – and those Bolsheviks

In the Second World War the Russians went from being evil collaborators with Hitler, to
being our gallant allies. In the First World War it was the other way round. It was
announced that 19 May 1917 was to be a Russian flag day in Reading, with the aim of
endowing a Reading bed in an Anglo-Russian hospital. The timing was somewhat
unfortunate; the Tsar had just abdicated and Lenin had arrived back in Russia, to
precipitate the Bolshevik revolution that would lead to Russia's withdrawal from the
war. How much this affected the generosity of the Reading public is not clear, but the
flag day raised just £137 11*s*, about a quarter of the expected sum.

Their subsequent peace negotiations with Germany brought a predictable editorial
response from the British press:

Bolshevism betrays Britain

*Bolshevism, having had a good innings and played the war game according to its
peculiar notions, has thrown up the sponge and acknowledged that it cannot win
in its own fashion. But when it comes down to rock bottom there is no denying
the fact that the action of its leaders is simply a gross betrayal of Britain and its
allies. It is also a betrayal of the working classes of this country, because it has
thrown on them, amongst others, the burden of the fight for liberty and
civilisation . . .*

*Unfortunately, there is only too much ground for suspicion that Lenin, Trotski
and Co. are playing a very elaborate comedy with the assistance of Germany.
The fact is after making a show of indignation at Germany's demands, they have
given away at every point.[16]*

For good measure, the editorial pointed out that some of them – Lenin in particular – had returned to Russia with the connivance of the Germans (and, they suggested, with German funding). This was only one of many editorial onslaughts against Bolshevism:

> *Bolshevism does not mean liberty and democracy, but despoliation and repression. It is as tyrannous as absolutism and even more so. Says Mr William Stephen Saunders, the Labour delegate to Russia 1917: 'Bolsheviks are the exponents of physical force, which they use not only against landlords and capitalists, but also against Socialists who do not agree with their anarchic and terrorising proceedings. Under Bolshevism all political liberties are really suppressed and life is wantonly taken.'[17]*

These views also found their way into domestic politics. There was a dispute between two rival would-be Labour parliamentary candidates, one of whom happened to express some sympathy for the Bolshevik cause. Worse still, he happened to come from Wales, prompting this outburst against the principality:

> *The whole region is seething with disloyalty, and dominated by petty Lenins and Trotzkys [sic], whose policy is peace with Germany by means of negotiations, in order that a ruthless class war may be fought to a finish . . . Give them their way, and the industry they intend to control will pillage and oppress all other classes of the community.[18]*

The instruments of war

Britain's unprecedentedly vast standing Army generated a need for every kind of war material. British machine-gun output, which stood at just 274 in 1914, rose to 120,864 by 1918, and there were comparably huge orders for everything from Army uniforms, through mess-tin covers, canvas buckets and horse bandages, to 137 million pairs of socks. But, most of all, the development of quick-firing heavy guns created a voracious demand for shells. Britain would supply some 187 million shells to the Western Front by the end of the war. The manufacture of these munitions was not only unpleasant, but also highly dangerous. It turned the skin of the workers yellow, leading to their nickname – 'canaries' – and caused nausea and chest pains. Some 400 women munitions workers were killed from exposure to TNT. However, the Government strongly resisted any suggestion that munitions work was hazardous to health:

> *The attention of the Minister of Munitions has been drawn to the fact that persistent rumours, possibly of enemy origin, are in circulation as to the danger to the life of men and women employed in national filling factories. These rumours are most misleading and are affecting the labour supply to new factories.*

Experts were called upon to offer the following reassurance:

> *High Explosives may cause skin irritation. This, however, is not a danger to life and does not persist when the work is discontinued or changed. TNT is the explosive which may cause illness but out of the many thousands coming into*

contact with it the number seriously or fatally attacked has been limited to a few isolated cases . . .

the spreading of such false rumours at a time like this can only be attributed to sinister or unpatriotic motives.[19]

More to the point, it could earn you a huge fine or six months' imprisonment under the DORA regulations. One man who would draw no comfort from the official reassurance was Robert Graham (aged 39). He had been a munitions worker for some time, and had been complaining that exposure to TNT was making him ill. He managed to get a few days off work but, on the train home from London, his condition worsened. By the time medical help got to him, he was dead. The post-mortem found the classic signs of TNT poisoning – his fingers, eyebrows and scalp were all stained yellow – and the cause of death was given as syncope (heart failure) due to a fatty heart. This again could have been the result of TNT poisoning but, because they did not feel able to make the causal link with absolute certainty (or more likely did not want to deter anyone from working in munitions), the Coroner's jury returned a verdict of death by natural causes. Such verdicts lead one to wonder how far the official numbers of TNT-related deaths were an under-estimate.

But a more immediate hazard to health with TNT was the risk of being blown up. In part, at least, this seems to have been due a terrifyingly casual attitude towards explosives on the part of some of the munitions workers:

a communication had been received from the Home Office, stating that notwithstanding the special measures taken for the purpose of preventing employees from bringing matches into and smoking in explosive factories, these illegal and dangerous practices were still widely prevalent, and the situation was one to cause the Government grave concern. The Home Secretary pointed out that it involved great and immediate danger to the lives of the employees and of the public, also a menace to national safety.[20]

The very day after the newspaper carried this report, just the kind of disaster the Home Secretary envisaged occurred in London. Silvertown was an area of east London developed by one Samuel Winkworth Silver in the 1850s. Falling just outside that part of London where business activities were more tightly regulated, it became the home for a variety of more or less noxious industries, setting cheek by jowl with densely packed slum housing. Brunner Mond (a forerunner of Imperial Chemical Industries) set up a plant there, part of which was standing idle after 1912. By 1915, the Government was facing a massive shortfall in munitions production, and decided to use the site for the purification of the explosive TNT. Brunner objected; this was an immensely dangerous activity, one wholly unsuited to a densely packed residential area. But under pressure from the Government they yielded, and production started in September 1915.

On 19 January 1917, a fire broke out in the melt pot room of the works. Fire-fighters were called, and were tackling the blaze when, at 6.52pm, about 50 tons of TNT exploded. The resulting fire was seen as far away as Maidstone and Guildford and the explosion heard in Southampton and Norwich. Red-hot debris was strewn for miles around; some of it pierced a gasholder on the opposite bank of the Thames, and a fireball of 7.1 million cubic feet of gas added to the conflagration. The *Stratford Express* described the scene of devastation:

The whole heavens were lit in awful splendour. A fiery glow seemed to have come over the dark and miserable January evening and objects which a few minutes before had been blotted out in the intense darkness were silhouetted against the sky.[21]

As a result 900 houses and about 17 acres of warehousing were destroyed or badly damaged. Between 60,000 and 70,000 homes were damaged to some degree. There were 73 people killed and over 400 injured, a relatively low figure given the potential for loss of life in an area like this. Dark rumours circulated about it being the result of enemy sabotage or an air raid, but an inquiry failed to establish a definitive cause (they did, however, conclude that the area was an unsuitable place to be carrying out such a process, and that safety procedures at the factory were unsatisfactory). The inquiry's report, which was completed within about a month of the explosion, was not made public until the 1950s.

War crimes

The extension of state control into every area of people's lives also created rich opportunities for the fertile criminal mind. At the outbreak of war, Government officials went around requisitioning large numbers of horses, with which to carry the Expeditionary Force to the enemy. But not all of those doing the requisitioning were

Government officials. There were enough criminals falsely requisitioning horses for distinctly non-military purposes for the Government to issue a warning; do not hand over your horse to anyone, unless he is accompanied by a policeman, or has the necessary official paperwork to support the requisition (though how the average citizen was supposed to distinguish between the official papers and a fraudulent imitation was an unanswered question). Cases were also reported (and officially denied) of over-zealous officials stopping ladies in mid-journey and leaving them stranded in the street, deprived of their carriage horses.

The Archdeacon of Winchester had a Church-owned property in the Cathedral Close commandeered at short notice as a war hospital, allegedly based on 'secret despatches'. When the Archdeacon had occasion to query some aspect of this with the War Office, they denied all knowledge of the arrangement. The Archdeacon hurried back to the property, only to find it ransacked but vacant, with no clue left behind as to the perpetrator of the crime.

One Allen Bowen perpetrated an even more ambitious fraud. He presented himself at the premises of a tool manufacturer in Manchester's Newton Heath, claiming to be an official from the Ministry of Munitions. On this basis, he took over effective control of the company, installing himself in an office there, controlling all inbound and outbound correspondence and taking over the hiring and firing of staff. (In relation to hiring and firing, one of his first appointments was himself, putting himself on the payroll at a salary of £5 a week.) His reign of terror lasted for eleven weeks, until his behaviour became so obnoxious that the company plucked up the courage to complain about him to the Ministry. They disavowed all knowledge of Mr Bowen and he quickly exchanged the life of an entrepreneur for one at His Majesty's Pleasure.

One way in which the Army addressed the problem of housing its growing numbers of soldiers was by billeting them on private citizens. But it seems such arrangements were also open to fraud, for the authorities found it necessary to warn householders not to accept soldiers for billeting unless the individual was accompanied by a police officer, or was in possession of a blue billeting form. Failure to do so could put them at risk and they could expect no payment for it.

Some practised fraud for no obvious financial gain. Sir Douglas Edward Scott, Baronet, sounded like a member of the officer class, and was dressed as a naval Commander when he was arrested in Buckingham Palace Road. The only problem was that he was actually a clerk in holy orders. He could offer no explanation for this breach of dress code (or at least none that the newspaper revealed to its readers) when he appeared before the magistrates. It appears that he may have had a more general difficulty in dealing with reality, given that he was twice declared bankrupt while holding clerical posts. His arrest on this occasion may well have had something to do with the fact that he was imprisoned for bigamy later in 1918.

The Royal Family

The Royal Family were keen to be associated with the war effort. Initially they were – but unfortunately rather too strongly with the other side. The family name, Saxe-Coburg, had rather too much of a Hanoverian flavour to it for most patriotic tastes. But it was not just the name that raised questions about whose side they were on:

Princess Christian and the Duchess of Albany will receive the sympathy of every woman in the country, in their sad position created by the war. The former lost a son in the Boer campaign, and as their only surviving son is a major in the Prussian army – being heir to the Duchy of Schleswig-Holstein – he will be called upon to fight against the country of his birth. The same lot has fallen to the Duchess of Albany, whose only son, the reigning Duke of Saxe-Coburg-Gotha, has had to send his contingent to the German forces. He is married to a German princess and has several children. The Brother of the Duchess, the Prince of Waldeck-Pyrmont, is also fighting with the army of the Kaiser.[22]

So it was in April 1917 that *The Times* announced that the Royal Family were renouncing all links with foreign orders and changing the family name to Windsor. They also wished to be seen to be working for the cause:

The Queen and Princess Mary are actively preparing comforts for the soldiers at the front. On Wednesday her Majesty spent several hours in Princess Mary's sitting room and cut out shirts which the Princess hemmed with a sewing machine.[23]

One thing that was not discontinued for the duration was the sycophantic coverage of any royal visit by the local press:

This is the first time King George has paid a visit to Reading since he ascended the throne, and both he and his consort gave unmistakeable proof that they were deeply impressed at the people's splendid welcome. This they repeatedly acknowledged, the Queen not only bowing, but several times waving her hand.[24]

Recycling

By 1917, the sorts of campaigns normally associated with the Second World War, to stop people wasting anything, were getting under way. Supplies of wood pulp for paper-making were down to a third of their pre-war level, making it vital to recycle every scrap of paper. Girl Guides made this part of their war effort. Scrap iron was also needed, not least to replace the tonnage of shipping being lost to the submarines. Another target was bones and animal fats. These were a useful source of glycerine, needed in the manufacture of munitions. The public were regaled with fascinating facts, such as that 2½ pounds of waste fat yields enough raw material to make an 18-pounder shell. It was reported that Lady Anderson of Wimbledon was doing her bit, by saving her washing-up water, cooling it and skimming the fat off it. Quite what her household (of five people) were eating beggars the imagination for, in just five days, this process allegedly yielded nearly a pound of solid pure white fat. One rather odd appeal, launched in 1918, was for fruit stones and nut shells. It seemed that these, reduced to charcoal, were ideal for the manufacture of gas masks. Another unexpected source of munition materials was the humble conker, and the authorities appealed for anyone with horse-chestnut trees on their land to get in touch and let them come and collect them. Up and down the country, schoolchildren were despatched on conker hunts and Wiltshire proudly boasted that 287 of its schools had together collected 110 tons (well above the county average of 65 tons).

But, if the propagandists were to be believed, the Germans were well ahead of us in the recycling stakes. Reports were coming in of *Kadaver* factories, and dark suggestions were being made that it was not just the bodies of dead animals from the battlefield that were being recycled into soap and fertiliser.

The hand of officialdom

One thing that was never in short supply in the war years was Government advice, exhortation and instruction (some of it frequently changeable). The Government recognised that the public were becoming bewildered by it all and, in 1918, launched a series of Government Information Bureaux in branches of Boots the Chemists up and down the country. There, people who were in any doubt as to what their obligations as a wartime citizen were could seek advice on any matter. The crowds visiting one branch during its opening week certainly tested the breadth of the staff's knowledge, with questions about everything from National Service to cooking hints.

DORA (the regulations under the Defence of the Realm Act, introduced at the outbreak of war) interfered with the lives of citizens in a multitude of different ways, great and small. Among the great ways were the introduction of rationing, conscription and the curtailment of the civil liberties of enemy aliens. Some of the small ones provoked irritation, or even ridicule, as in this editorial:

> *DORA is responsible for another benevolent form of despotism. No reference must now be made to the weather, in case information may be conveyed to the enemy . . . As the Newbury Weekly News does reach the front lines, and may fall into hostile hands, care must be observed not to hint when the sun shines, the rain falls or the wind blows at Newbury. Such views might have dire consequences, and there is always the personal possible six months' imprisonment, or a fine of £100, or both.*[25]

A following week's editorial began satirically:

> *Whitsuntide's weather was — — — (deleted). Well, if it cannot be said, there is at least satisfaction in recollection...*[26]

Not even the goodwill generated by the Armistice would persuade this editor to bury the hatchet with the administrators of DORA:

> *DORA is not dead but dozeth and, like a watch-dog, has one eye open. There are some things we may now do without having to appear before the magistrates, with the chance of £100, or six months, or both. We may light half the street*

lamps, if we can get the coal to make the gas. We can leave our blinds undrawn if
we choose. Possibly we can make some reference to that good old topic, the
weather. DORA has ordered that the masking of street lamps may be removed,
but in view of the coal shortage, the total number of lamps in use should not
exceed one-half. The shading of lights in houses may be withdrawn, but the
prohibition of lights in shop windows and advertisement lights must be
maintained on account of the coal shortage. The restrictions on the ringing of
bells and striking of public clocks at night are withdrawn. We may even indulge
in bonfires and fireworks under police directions.[27]

The war atrocities committed by the Germans were subject to the full glare of Allied
publicity, but what of those committed by the British Government? This correspondent
had no intention of letting them off the hook over one outrage. He wanted to know:

how the authorities more particularly concerned could have so lost their normal
mental equilibrium as to support the perpetration of such an atrocity?[28]

The atrocity he was referring to was the commandeering of the British and Natural
History Museums for the war effort, something which would in his view lead to
irreparable loss and damage of specimens while they were being decanted. Another group
of residents was up in arms at a desecration to the natural environment being committed
in the name of the war effort:

The residents of Wash Common are in a state of great consternation at finding
that the beautiful group of Scotch firs growing on the burial grounds of what was
formerly Enborn Heath are marked for destruction, the purpose being to convert
them into pit props or some other government purpose. Some of these fine old
trees are actually growing upon the soldiers' graves, evidently having been
planted there as memorials and standing like sentinels over these last resting
places of the brave men who fell fighting in the first battle of Newbury. The
affections of the people of Newbury have always clung around the graves where
the bodies of Cavalier and Roundhead lie side by side.[29]

Appeals

No sooner were hostilities declared than the campaigns to provide comforts for our brave
boys started to appear. The local paper was soon awash with appeals to support one aspect
or another of the war effort. One appeal that achieved a high profile was 'Smokes for
Soldiers and Sailors', whose aim was to provide the forces with tobacco (as if they did
not have enough health hazards to contend with on the Western Front). Readers were
given piteous stories of our deprived boys smoking tree bark, straw and dried grass.
Among the appeal's (to modern eyes unlikely) champions was the Red Cross, and the
medical journal the *Lancet* also waxed lyrical about the merits of tobacco:

To the soldier . . . with his nervous system in a ceaseless state of tension from the
dangers and excitement, tobacco must be a real solace and joy.[30]

Indeed, all patriotic Britons should take up the habit for tax reasons:

Smoking used to be a luxury merely, now it is a duty, for of every 1s paid for tobacco at 4d an ounce, considerably over a half, or about 8d represents tax . . . Therefore smokers should smoke more, rather than less.[31]

It was perhaps timely that, the same week, the French Academy of Science reported new research showing that it was possible to survive with only one sixth of a lung.

On every side, the newspaper reader was assailed with suggestions of comforts to send to their loved ones in the trenches, from soap, cigarettes and food, to patent medicines and layer upon layer of clothing in which to swaddle themselves. One paper suggested a compact emergency kit for soldiers, consisting of:

- mercurial ointment 'to keep the body clear of a scourge only too well-known to old campaigners';
- carbolic soap;
- extra emergency rations (small jars of meat extract);
- matches in a watertight tin;
- a darning kit for socks; and
- a tin of Vaseline, for which diverse uses were suggested.

Scarcely a week went by without the local paper carrying an appeal from one front-line troop or another with local connections for some form of comfort. These could range from prosaic things like warm socks and balaclavas, through entertainments – footballs, books and magazines, and gramophones and the records to play on them were particularly popular – to the slightly bizarre. One group of soldiers wanted wigs, fancy dress and theatrical props, to enable them to stage theatrical entertainments. (Also, if anyone had any comic sketches, these would also be gratefully received.)

But those seeking a really deserving case needed to look no further than the 7th Supernumary Company. They needed cricket sets and games, since they had been entrusted with the task of guarding the railways of Hampshire and the work was 'very monotonous and dull'. They were even reduced to sleeping, not under fire in muddy trenches, but in stations and spare railway carriages.

The rapid turnover of officers meant good business for military outfitters.

Chapter 9

The Demon Drink

We are fighting Germany, Austria and drink and as far as I am concerned, the greatest of these foes is drink.

David Lloyd George
January 1915

Please don't ask the recruits to have a drink in this house. They don't need 'Dutch courage'. Their uniform proves this.

Recruits – Don't go beyond your one glass, and pay for that yourself. Most of those that would treat you are those who haven't the pluck to follow your example – and enlist.

Notice in a South Wales pub

'Whiskey, my friend, has killed more men than bullets'
'That may be, sir, but I'd rather be full of whiskey than bullets'.

Joke © 1915

The role of alcohol in the life of the nation was one of the big debates of the Great War. Those in the temperance movement thought it should play no part at all. Those in the Anti-Treating Leagues (or looking to set one up locally) had more limited concerns about treating, where the practice of buying rounds of drinks for others (particularly members of the armed forces) was felt to lead to excessive consumption. Politicians were concerned about the localised effects that alcohol was having on munitions production. Those in the brewing industry, and a large proportion of their customers, shared none of these concerns, and were more interested in, respectively, their profits and their thirsts.

From the earliest days of the war the temperance movement pushed the authorities for the earlier closure of pubs. In an open letter to the local Magistrates, these campaigners seemed to attach greatest importance to the moral danger faced by soldiers' wives:

Very regrettable results follow from the well-intentioned but dangerous custom of treating soldiers in our midst; and a large number of women are now exposed to greater temptations to drink – partly on account of suddenly handling more money than they are accustomed to receive, and partly on account of the loneliness and anxiety of their position.

All the circumstances of war combine to create special temptations to resort to intoxicating drink. Patriotic ardour leads to excitement on the part of those leaving home, and the derangement of the usual habits of life on the part of those remaining at home, accompanied as it is by nervous strain, leads to depression. In either case, resort to the public house is a frequent result, and the people concerned are much less able than usual to practice moderation and restraint.[1]

Before the war, many respectable women would not be seen on licensed premises, particularly alone, for fear of being mistaken as prostitutes. One 'well-dressed young woman' had no such inhibitions; she thought she had entered a hostelry, but when she demanded service, she was immediately arrested for drunkenness. In her already befuddled state, she had mistaken the police station for a pub.

For their part, the licensed victuallers opposed earlier closing which, in their view, would lead to a collapse of the moral fibre of the nation. It would:

- lead to immorality;
- lead to more private and home drinking;
- encourage gambling;
- lead to many pubs closing altogether; and they also argued that
- recent Government impositions on the industry would achieve the desired reduction in consumption, in any event.

Other protesters threw a whole raft of new arguments against restricted opening. It was biased against the poor, since the rich had the facilities for drinking at home; it would encourage people to go straight from work to the pub, undermining family life; the closure would be too early in the evening, and would result in drunks wandering the streets; it would make little difference to military clientele, who had to be back in their quarters by 9.30 in any event. Equally infuriated were the political clubs, who relied on their bar takings to cross-subsidise their good works in the community, and who had to keep open all evening, regardless of whether they were making any money from it. As they pointed out, they together represented every shade of political opinion (apart from the rabidly teetotal). Liverpool licensed victuallers also cited evidence from Government Commissions that the lack of a reasonable supply of alcoholic refreshment for the working classes was proving to be a powerful cause of industrial unrest.

In Wokingham, the magistrates decreed that town pubs should shut by 10.00pm and rural ones by 9.00pm. The magistrates (and the local paper) were at pains to try and avoid this casting aspersions on the drinking habits of our brave lads:

their [the magistrates'] action should not be considered to have relation to the behaviour of soldiers in the past or what was anticipated in the future. They simply 'thought it well' that there should be an earlier closing.[2]

If anyone were to be blamed, the paper suggested, it should be the 'undesirable camp followers' that soldiers seemed to attract in wartime, repeatedly toasting the health of Tommy Atkins and his fellows, and plying the (normally totally abstemious) soldiers with liquor. Abolitionists sometimes liked to contrast the sporting battlefield behaviour of 'Tommy the Teetotaller' with the drink-fuelled bestiality of the German forces. One lobbyist even went so far as to claim that German spies were promoting treating, as a means of crippling our munitions production and impoverishing the workforce.

But the abolitionists' praise for our brave lads was not unqualified, as this editorial broadside against the teetotal cause shows:

Another sore point with the bigots is the issue of a small quantity of rum to the troops on active service. Such people might radically change their views if they were forced to spend days together in rain-soaked trenches with little sleep and insufficient food. As it is, it can only be supposed that none of them has experienced the rigours of strenuous warfare.[3]

Yet another correspondent was at pains to deny that the soldiers' tot was anything other than medicinal:

It is not generally known that rum is an almost certain preventative against colds when a man gets soaked to the skin with rain and has to keep his clothes on for hours. No man outside a lunatic asylum would dream that rum was being served out to the troops other than as a medicine.[4]

As the battle over pub licensing hours continued, the licensed victuallers went over the magistrates' head to the Home Secretary. He told them that not even he had powers to grant an extension. An early case of a breach of the new regulations came before the courts in January 1915, when what appears to have been a rather officious police officer observed a man leaving a pub at just 11 minutes past 9, carrying a jug of beer. A prosecution ensued, but the officer was unable to produce evidence of after-hours sales. The man with the jug claimed he had bought the beer before 9.00pm and had been engaged in conversation since. None of the regulars were about to testify against the licensee, and the case was dismissed. This was, perhaps, a false dawn for the licensed trade for, in most future cases, the magistrates were far more likely to believe the arresting officers' story than that of the pub's customers.

Temperance preacher Tennyson Smith addressed a meeting (presumably of the already converted) at the YMCA and sought inspiration from overseas:

People who 'treated' soldiers were far greater foes to this country than any German spy, and a far greater danger . . . For the Tsar, with one stroke of his pen, to abolish the use of alcohol in Russia, was one of the most wonderful things that had ever happened, and Great Britain was going to do the same one day.[5]

In fact, what the Tsar had decreed was the much more limited step of banning the manufacture and consumption of vodka for the duration (with much more temporary restrictions on other alcohol), and there was considerable scepticism among subsequent correspondents to the paper about his chances of making even that happen. Their scepticism was well-placed; the main consequence of the Tsar closing 400 state-run distilleries and 28,000 spirit shops was that the Russian public began making their own moonshine in large quantities and Government tax revenues fell by 30 per cent. One correspondent, not himself an advocate of teetotalism, could nonetheless see some good in the Tsar's action:

Many references have been made by speakers to this subject, but not one of them has explained what vile stuff Russian 'vodka' really is. It is an exceptionally strong spirit and was consumed by the Russians (before the war) in vast quantities. In fact there is nothing to compare to it in this country and all moderate men are of the opinion that curtailing its sale will be a good thing for the inhabitants.[6]

Equally understated in their claims about alcohol were the Templars, who also called for a total ban on alcohol, claiming that it had led to 'rioting and violent deaths and presented an insurmountable barrier to complete efficiency and public order'. A correspondent named 'Teetotaller' agreed:

We all know something of the destruction of life and property caused by this war; we have all read something of the houses and farms and crops and towns shelled and burned; we all know something of the awful loss of life, not only of soldiers, but of women and children. Yet tremendous and horrible as is that carnage, it is but a trifle compared with the havoc wrought by drink.[7]

Field Marshal Douglas Haig had his own radical solution to the problem of intemperance:

I suspect that the New Army has taken away a very large number of the best workers, so that many who were only occasional workers (because of their taste for drink) have now to work full time. Their presence or absence was hardly noticed until the need for a full output of work was rendered necessary by the war . . . The best thing, in my opinion, is to punish some of the chief offenders . . . Take and shoot two or three of them, and the 'drink habit' would cease, I feel sure.[8]

Another military leader, the recently deceased Lord Roberts, had taken an entirely different view of temperance. During his lifetime, he:

did not agree with the total abstainer but had great faith in the soldier who was temperate in all things. He considered the soldier who drank moderately a finer character than he who took the pledge, because the latter could not trust himself to take stimulants.[9]

But why did men drink? In his newly published book *John Barleycorn* Jack London sought to explain:

we drink mainly because of the accessibility of alcohol; that it has become by custom and habit an essential adjunct of social intercourse that in his case it was only by drinking, and drinking hard, that he could prove himself a man, mix with his equals and betters and make progress in the adventurous career he had chosen to adopt as an alternative to practical slavery in a factory . . .[10]

His sole remedy for this problem was prohibition, a solution that he felt would inflict no hardship on the next generation.

By May 1915, the brewing industry had yet more to complain about, as the Government proposed further tax rises on alcohol as an aid to increasing munitions production. The Allied Brewery Traders' Association railed against what they described as 'prohibition by taxation', complaining that they had already suffered a 25 per cent drop in trade, following the last tax increase:

> *it spells ruination to some of the largest brewers in the country, to say nothing of the many trades allied to the brewing industry . . . We are convinced that the whole agitation is the outcome of the Temperance party taking advantage of the necessities of the war to wreak its will, through the Government, on a trade which has been established, maintained, taxed, regulated and controlled by successive governments for hundreds of years.[11]*

It would get worse still for the brewers. In February 1916, the Defence of the Realm Act was used to impose even stricter limits over the sale of drink across wide areas of the country:

> *on the grounds that war material is being made, loaded, unloaded and dealt with in transit therein, and that men belonging to His Majesty's Naval and military forces are assembled therein.[12]*

Across large areas of the country, some of which had only the most tenuous connection with the criteria laid down in the regulations, this meant opening hours of pubs being limited to 12.00–2.30pm and 6.00–9.00pm (Monday to Saturday) and 12.30–2.30pm and 6.00–9.00pm (Sunday). Off-sales were even more strictly controlled, with closing time being called at 8.00pm. Under the same regulations, treating also became illegal, potentially carrying a penalty of six months in gaol. Some, like the *Spectator* magazine, thought this was an excellent idea, which would 'free hundreds of thousands of men from an expensive and senseless social tyranny' in which working men felt under an obligation to buy everyone else in their group a drink. However, the licensed trade was predictably furious about the treating ban, which opened so many avenues for evasion. As one licensee put it:

> *Speaking broadly, I say that this no treating business is utterly useless, as it is open to so much evasion. Another thing I should like to point out is that there is nothing in the Order that will prevent any person staying in the town in a temperance hotel from procuring any intoxicating liquor, taking it to the hotel and inviting his friends to partake.[13]*

Membership clubs, where only members could get served at the bar, faced an even more ridiculous situation. Members' guests could not get a drink at all, unless they were treated.

As an example of the law on treating being taken to its ridiculous extreme, the *Morning Post* in March 1916 carried a report about one Robert Smith being fined for buying his wife a glass of wine in a pub. For good measure, Mrs Smith was also fined £1 for drinking it, and the barmaid £5 for serving it. Smith had claimed unsuccessfully in his defence that his wife had given him 6*d* to pay for it. Up in Newcastle, a licensee had a novel solution to the treating problem; when a customer ordered eight drinks, the landlord insisted that he drank them all himself, in front of witnesses, to prove that it was not a round. Not even Tottenham Hotspurs captain Bobbie Steel was exempt. He was fined 50*s* for buying his brother-in-law a sherry, under the misapprehension that it was non-alcoholic (his brother-in-law was teetotal).

Part of the problem was that the wages of working people, particularly in the war industries, had gone up so much that two or three days' work would keep them in drinking money for a whole week. As a Newcastle shipbuilder put it, a double shift on a Sunday meant no attendance on Monday. This problem was particularly acute in the areas where war production was concentrated. One such example was at Gretna, on the Scottish border, where a giant munitions factory was established, employing some 15,000 people, many of them Irish immigrants. The incidence of drunkenness offences in the surrounding area increased four-fold. The Government's response was to buy up as many as possible of the area's pubs and breweries. In nearby Carlisle they closed 48 of the town's 119 pubs, and banned the advertising of alcohol and the sale of spirits on Saturdays. They also gave the nation that ultimate deterrent to drinking, the state-run pub, later described as being:

About as cheerful in appearance as an undertaker's shop, in the hands of the official receiver on a wet day.[14]

Attempts were made to apply the state restriction principle elsewhere. The Assistant Provost Marshal of the Aldershot Command, Colonel F. Dorling, turned up to a meeting of the Wokingham Magistrates in February 1917, with an alarming proposal that at least half the 150-odd licensed premises in their jurisdiction should be closed down. This was due not to any specific misbehaviour on the part of either the landlords or their customers, but rather on a view that his men should not be exposed to the temptation. Once the Magistrates had had a chance to digest this bombshell, they told the Colonel that they did not have the powers to do so and that, in any event, there would be serious issues of compensation involved. (No doubt the all-encompassing powers of the Defence of the Realm Act would have given the Government the legal means of doing so, but the Magistrates had no stomach for being at the vanguard of such a controversial move.)

There were even calls for the Government to nationalise the brewing industry and its retail outlets throughout the land. Manchester Statistical Society received a paper from a Mr R.B. Batty in January 1917, advocating just such a measure as a step towards temperance reform, by removing the political power of the brewing industry. He claimed it would also yield substantial efficiency savings, for example by doing away with competitive advertising. Some prohibitionists initially gave at least two cheers for the idea, but then thought more carefully about its ramifications. What they wanted was the abolition of the drinks industry, not its regulation. Nationalisation would make everyone in the country a stakeholder in the profits from alcohol, which might make prohibition harder, not easier, to secure. For the Government, the substantial cost of compulsorily purchasing the industry (something the war economy could ill afford) would create a sore temptation to promote rather than restrict alcohol sales, to recoup their outlay.

One correspondent had little time for those in the teetotal movement who called for prohibition. In his view, you were likely to find a much higher proportion of prohibitionists among the pacifists, conscientious objectors and pro-Germans. They were:

by no means so keen to win the war by prohibition as they are to win prohibition by exploiting the exigencies of the war.

By contrast:

The overwhelming majority of our fighting men . . . are honest gentlemen, good patriots and moderate drinkers.[15]

As the numbers of wounded personnel coming back from the front steadily increased, a new trap emerged to ensnare the incautious landlord. It seemed that numbers of servicemen still being treated for their wounds were managing to get out to the pub and prescribe their own alcoholic cures. These, the authorities said, would hinder their convalescence, make them more prone to future infection and less likely to make a full recovery from it. In the worst case, a landlord serving a patient who then expired for whatever reason could potentially be guilty of murder. The magistrates could hand out penalties of up to a £100 fine or six months in gaol to any licensee committing the offence. Worse still, the onus was placed on the landlord to ensure that his customers were not patients still undergoing treatment. One person who fell foul of this rule was a cleaner at Stockport Hospital, one Eva Dealey. She was observed buying beer from a pub and taking it home, where one of the patients from her ward was found to be visiting. The gallant soldier insisted that the beer was purely for Ms Dealey, and that he was only visiting for the pleasure of her company. This did not explain why his breath smelt of beer.

Lloyd George was behind a campaign of leading by example, whereby he persuaded leading public figures to foreswear alcohol for the duration of the war. The Royal Household and Secretary of State for War Lord Kitchener were two prominent signatories to the campaign. But Prime Minister Asquith, who had, let us say, a well-developed thirst (he was known to his parliamentary colleagues – behind his back – as 'squiffy'), declined to take part. But it was perhaps successive hikes in the duty on alcohol that did most to curb the nation's consumption. By the end of 1916, the cost of the barley needed to make alcohol had risen to roughly twice its pre-war level and the quantity available for brewing and distilling had roughly halved, as more and more barley was diverted into bread production.

In 1917, the Food Controller caused further outrage among beer drinkers by announcing a further 30 per cent cut in production, ostensibly to save on materials that could otherwise be used for food production, and on transport costs. A correspondent, writing under the name of 'Civis', complained to his local paper, demanding to know why similar restrictions had not been placed on tea and coffee, two other stimulants with no food value. He cited the French, who had commandeered the entire vintage of their wine production for the consumption of their troops, claiming that:

the daily consumption of wine has contributed in a very material degree to the magnificent health which all ranks have enjoyed since the beginning of the war.

He went on to point out that even the Germans and our own Government saw a regular supply of beer as essential to their soldiers' well-being, and argued that:

What is essential to the health of the army cannot be regarded as a superfluity in the diet of the civilian population, especially in times of mental and physical strain.[16]

From February 1917, the malting of barley for alcohol production was banned entirely.

Brewers were left to depend upon existing stocks, which were only enough to produce 10 million barrels (compared with the pre-war level of over 36 million, or even the 26 million produced in the tightly constrained year up to March 1917. Even the 26 million represented less than half a pint per adult per day). In vain did the licensed trade restate the burdens that were being placed on it – not only was production restricted, but the tax on beer had been raised from 7*s* 9*d* to 25*s* a barrel, the cost of raw materials had increased by 300 per cent and the opening hours of pubs reduced from 17 a day to 5½ (4½ on Sundays).

Just to add to their troubles, in the latter part of the war, the watery product brewers were compelled to produce went by the heart-warming name of Government Beer. Brewers were worried lest this product sullied their reputation, and at least one felt the need to advertise the fact:[17]

NOTICE.

OWING to some misconception we think it well to state that we manufacture none of NICHOLSON'S BEER at present, but give the PUBLIC as GOVERNMENT BEER, the best article possible under the restrictions.

NICHOLSON & SONS, Ltd.,

THE BREWERY,

MAIDENHEAD.

One brewer looks to disassociate himself from the watery beer the Government forces him to brew.

November 1917 saw a small glimmer of hope for the brewing industry. The Beer (Output and Descriptions) Order 1917 allowed brewers to increase the gravity and quality of the 'Government Ale' that they brewed. There had been a lot of complaints from the public about the 'thin-drinking character' of the beer being offered to them, and the extra strength and warmth of the new brew would be particularly welcome in winter. Pig farmers meanwhile complained that they were being denied cereals to feed their animals, while brewers were being given extra supplies to make their products.

A correspondent to the *Manchester City News* challenged the arguments about foodstuffs being diverted into alcohol production. He claimed that much of the sugar used in brewing was not fit for mainstream culinary use and in any event amounted to just 1½oz per person per week. If beer were given up as an accompaniment to meals, people would simply slake their thirsts with tea, coffee or other beverages containing as much, or more, sugar. He said the barley used in brewing was not fit for bread-making, and that very little of the waste products of the process was thrown away. It either went as cattle or poultry food or, in the case of yeast, to make yeast extract.

Sunday, 6 January 1918 was observed throughout the country as a day of prayer and thanksgiving, in order, as the Royal Proclamation set forth, 'that we may have the clearsightedness and strength necessary to the victory of our cause'. As part of this, 'the whole of the public houses in the locality closed throughout the day' – an action worthy of note, for even when a sovereign had been laid to rest they had never previously been known to close for the whole day. The King required that his Proclamation be read out in church services held that day, though congregations in the nation's hostelries were denied the opportunity of drinking a toast to it.

Even as the Armistice was announced, a final wartime blow for the drinker in Portsmouth was announced, from an unexpected source:

> *Immediately the news [of the Armistice] becoming known, the Executive of the Licensed Victuallers Association met, and decided it should be recommended, in the interests of good order and seemly conduct, that the sale of spirits should be suspended throughout the day, and furthermore, not to open in the evening. The recommendation was complied with and there was no licensed house open in the evening, at all events on the principal streets.[18]*

The demon strikes – up before the courts

Despite the obstacles placed in their way, the pressures of war could still drive some men to drink. John Cobbett was found by a police officer climbing lamp-posts, in pursuit of imaginary objects. The officer detected a hint of alcohol on his breath and Cobbett, of no fixed abode, found himself before the courts, facing a £5 fine or seven days in gaol for drunkenness. Meanwhile, some of our brave allies were displaying their fighting qualities – but not always in the right place. Canadian Private James Singleton was found surrounded by a crowd, which he was entertaining with a virtuoso display of expletives. Attempts to get him to go home were unavailing and when the police tried to arrest him he went berserk. Singleton explained to the court that this had been the first time he had touched liquor. The little drop he had tried, coupled with the effects of being gassed on the Western Front, had 'made his head go wrong'. The magistrates were slightly more impressed with this defence than with Mr Cobbett's imaginary objects, in that they fined Singleton just £3.

Chapter 10
Bread and Circuses

Sport and war

There was a time for all things in the world. There was a time for games, there was a time for business and there was a time for domestic life. There was a time for everything, but there is only time for one thing now, and that thing is war. If the cricketer had a straight eye, let him look along the barrel of a rifle. If a footballer had strength of limb, let them serve and march on the field of battle.

Arthur Conan Doyle
6 September 1914

Should sport continue at all in a time of war? Lord Roberts was quoted in the papers, agreeing with Conan Doyle that 'this is no time for sport'. This prompted a lively debate and this local paper summed up the issues:

The war and sport: are games to continue?

With England engaged in the most gigantic war the world has ever seen, a great diversity of opinion exists as to whether games should continue to be permitted to continue at home. There is no doubt that sport all over the country is suffering. Many people have not the heart to indulge in the old recreations and amusements at this time of great national stress. In Reading there appears to be a unanimity of opinion that athletes who are eligible should at all events devote part of their time to preparing themselves for any call which may be made upon them and it is gratifying to know that many members of clubs for the promotion of various branches of sport have already enlisted. On the other hand, it must be remembered that athletic agencies can fulfil a useful purpose in keeping fit those who are not eligible to bear arms, and that healthy outdoor recreation is better for young people than loafing about at our street corners.[1]

Most local opinion took predictable sides. Mr Cox, of Perry and Cox, sports outfitters, wanted to see sport continue, to keep people fit and to steer their minds from morbid thoughts. He pointed out that his biggest demand for footballs was coming from serving soldiers. But the abolitionists got an unexpected ally, in the form of the secretary of the local athletic club, who called for all sport to be abandoned for the duration.

But different sports raised different issues in August 1914. Cricket and rugby were amateur affairs and could not resist their participants' wish to join the colours (and the cricket season was, in any event, nearly over). Top-class football, on the other hand, was professional, with most players on one-year renewable contracts. Without the legal imperative of conscription, players could not join the forces unless their clubs released them from those contracts. That, and the mistaken belief that the war would be over by Christmas, led the Football League to carry on with the 1914–15 League programme as usual. Their decision prompted some barbed wit from this editorial:

The Football League management committee – which governs association football – yesterday decided that there shall be 'football as usual'. The Kaiser is now no doubt calling together his war staff to consider the crisis. England will fight for her life – on the football field. We will terrify the Germans with a display of our muscular youth, vociferously cheered on by thousands of the sons of Britain, who will pay their expenses to gather round the arena.

Football is a great sport, a good preparation in physical training for all who take part in it. But of the crowds who will gather at our big sporting enclosures, how many will be there who should be on the drill ground?[2]

No doubt stung by such criticism, the Football League tried to demonstrate that it was at least doing something for the war effort:

Clubs will be requested to place grounds at the disposal of the War Office on days other than match days, for use as drill grounds.

Where football matches are played, arrangements will be made for well-known public men to address the players and spectators, urging men who are physically fit and otherwise able to enlist at once.

Where practicable, recruiting stations to be on the grounds. . . .

It is hoped that where matches are played to encourage enlistment, the whole of the net gate receipts will be given to a war relief fund.[3]

Attempts to use football grounds as recruitment agencies were not spectacularly successful, if the experience in Liverpool was anything to go by. Over 16,000 cards were given out at the Everton and Liverpool grounds and just over a thousand were even returned, most of them declining to volunteer for various reasons. The entire exercise yielded just 206 new recruits.

The League's decision to continue did not prevent the 17th Service (Football) Battalion of the Middlesex Regiment being formed in December 1914, though its membership was initially drawn largely from the amateur ranks. It would suffer grievous casualties, with 500 of its intake of about 600 men dying either during the war, or afterwards, from injuries sustained in it. Nor did it prevent continued pressure being applied on football to give up its stock of fit young men to the war effort. The Bishop of Chelmsford added his views during a visit to Bethnal Green:

He felt that the cry against professional football at the present time was right. He could not understand men who had any feeling, any respect for their country, men in the prime of life, taking large salaries at a time like this for kicking a ball about. It seemed to him something incongruous and unworthy.[4]

But this correspondent (pen name 'Old Woman') did not believe football should be singled out:

Surely cricketers, actors, singers, artists or any able-bodied young men, whether
or not they contribute to the pleasure of the nation, are equally bound to help
their country if needed. An actor, for example, is ministering to pleasure every
whit as much as a footballer![5]

Another correspondent also had a radically different view of the nation's sporting
priorities:

May I be allowed through your columns to raise my humble protest against the
spirit in which many people are facing the present situation in the country
districts. How different from the English way in the olden days! I am very far
from advocating any senseless and useless pleasures at a time like this, but when
we are told that the Guildford, Chertsey and Surrey Agricultural Association and
others are all abandoning their ploughing matches . . . and that hunting may be
altogether stopped in many parts of the country, then that is another matter.

But how different were our forefathers! Drake was playing bowls on Plymouth
Hoe when they told him of the arrival of the Spanish Armada – but he finished
his game. Wellington imported English foxhounds into the Peninsula during the
long wars there . . .

No, a panicky revulsion to funeral dullness throughout the countryside is not
the spirit in which our forefathers won their battles . . .

I am not advocating anything that would keep any of our manhood from
answering their country's call in her hour of need, such as for example of the
carrying out of the usual series of league football matches would almost
certainly entail, but, for those who are necessarily bound to remain behind from
various causes and reasons, I do advocate a certain amount of sober and sane
recreation.[6]

There was a lively debate during the Second World War about whether hunting should
be allowed to continue in wartime – anti-hunt groups in that war argued that the food
consumed by the horses and hounds could be better used feeding the human population,
or the farm animals that fed humans. In the First War, the arguments were different, with
no less a person than the War Minister, Lord Derby, intervening on the side of the
huntsmen. He wanted to see hunting continue as it: 'is necessary for the continuance of
breeding and raising of light horses suitable for cavalry work'. Rather less surprisingly,
the Committee of the Masters of Foxhounds Association also lent its support for at least
a qualified continuation of hunting – that 'cub hunting should continue and take place as
long as needed in order to kill as many foxes as necessary in the country, but that hunting
should not be looked upon from a sporting point-of-view until the war is over'. (This
appears to be saying that people could carry on hunting, provided they did not enjoy it?)
Where possible, the authorities felt that hunts should be maintained by those ineligible
for military service; but if it were not possible, Lord Derby felt it should be grounds for
a tribunal to exempt a man from conscription. But if foxes could find nothing to celebrate
in the outbreak of war, at least the grouse could give whatever passed in their circles as
three cheers:

War prevented sportsmen going out yesterday to celebrate the festival of the

Twelfth, and most of the Scottish shootings were without a single sportsman, while few guns were out on English moors. Many ghillies and beaters have joined the ranks, but a large number of men have been thrown out of employment.[7]

The Football League was eventually pressured into releasing unmarried professionals for military service. *Athletic News* saw this pressure very much in class-war terms:

The whole agitation is nothing less than an attempt by the ruling classes to stop the recreation on one day of the week of the masses . . . What do they care for the poor man's sport? The poor are giving their lives for this country in thousands. In many cases they have nothing else . . . These should, according to a small clique of virulent snobs, be deprived of the one distraction that they have had for over thirty years.[8]

This correspondent had a simple solution to the matter:

Our young men would be much better employed shooting Germans than shooting goals. The public should not patronise these football matches while this serious crisis in our national affairs is on. If there were no spectators there would be no play, as they don't play for sport but for dividends . . . Why not pass a short Bill through Parliament making it compulsory for all young men between the ages of 19 and 30 to serve with the colours as long as the war shall last?[9]

But, if the experience of Oxford City Football Club was anything to go by, the sheer practicality of maintaining professional football when many of your supporters and players have been posted overseas could present a real problem:

The fixture lacked nothing in attractiveness – save that it was not a competitive game – the weather was almost ideal, and it was the first match of the season. Yet, in place of the usual several hundreds of fervid enthusiasts, there were not more than two hundred, and most of these men of middle age, quiet and even decorous. The war clouds which have gathered over Europe had not escaped the City Football Club headquarters. One thing is quite certain; if City cannot command more support than that given them on Saturday they will voluntarily have to put up the shutters.[10]

By the 1915–16 season, football had become a very hand-to-mouth affair. Internationals, league and Challenge Cup tournaments were a thing of the past, and local matches could be arranged 'provided they did not interfere with anybody's war work'. Matches could only be played on Saturday afternoons, recognised holidays or early closing day, and no payments were to be made to players.

But an example of how sporting activity could be combined with the war effort surfaced in Henley in March 1918. Newspaper advertisements invited the public to go along to a charity football match between the local female munitions workers and the male instructors at the nearby Royal Flying Corps training school. The 1,500 or so spectators soon worked out that that this would be no run-of-the-mill game. The munitionettes arrived, looking (the reports said) 'very smart' in their team kit of munitions overalls and caps, although they did appear to be rather more numerous than convention

IN AID OF THE RED CROSS.

Under the Patronage of His Worship the Mayor of Henley.

WE WANT YOU TO SEE SOME SPORT.

Take Notice ☞ **A FOOTBALL TEAM** of **FEMALE MUNITION WORKERS**

(MESSRS. STUART TURNER, LTD.)

have challenged the Non-Commissioned Officers of the R.F.C. School of Instruction. · The Match will be played at **NORTHFIELD END**,

TO-MORROW

Saturday, March 9th.   Kick·off at 2.30 p.m.

COME ALONG.   BRING YOUR FRIENDS AND SEE THE MATCH OF THE SEASON.

ADMISSION: Minimum, 6d.; Maximum—No Limit.
Collection in the Grounds.

All Proceeds, without deduction, will be handed to the Local Branch of the Red Cross Society.

dictated. And so it proved to be: their line-up was listed as two goalkeepers, three backs, three halves and seven forwards. There was something odd, too, about the men's team. Could it be the fact that they were all in fancy dress, and included a cavalier, a matador, a jester and a 'nigger minstrel'? Even the officials departed from sartorial convention; the three (or possibly more – no one was quite sure) linesmen were also in fancy dress and the referee was made up as 'a typical coon'. Once the match (played in four 15-minute 'halves') got under way, according to the reports:

> *The fun waxed thick and fast all the way through, and put anything like a first-class exposition of the great winter pastime in the shade.*

But having said that:

> *It was seen at once that the girls were not quite novices, for some of them had a really good knowledge of the game, whilst the Flying Corps, despite that they were disguised by their costumes showed that, if called upon, they could give a*

first-class team a real gruelling. But they were not out to make goals, but to provide amusement.[11]

The officials cannot be said to have observed scrupulous neutrality. Dubious decisions were given in the munitionettes' favour and the referee was not even above kicking the ball their way. By the second 'half' the ladies led 2–0 (one of them scored from a highly questionable penalty award). Later in the game, one of the Royal Flying Corps team was stretchered off with a (prearranged and bogus) injury, which gave the 'ambulance men' an opportunity for some comical touchline 'first aid'. By the end of the match, the ladies were declared the winners by a score of 5–1 and over £100 had been raised for the Red Cross Hospital. Players and officials retired to the town for post-match celebrations, including a tea party and dance.

Entertainments

Unlike the opening weeks of the Second World War, theatres and other places of entertainment were allowed to continue uninterrupted in August 1914. One of the big variety attractions of the day was Mr Fred Karno's 'comedy concoctions' who, one reviewer assured us, would keep the audience amused from start to finish with their 'mirth producing propensities'. Karno's early claim to fame was the invention of the custard-pie-in-the-face routine. Shortly before the outbreak of war, one of its members quit for a job in America. Colleagues told him he was mad to give up regular work with

a well-known act for the uncertainties of the new-fangled moving picture industry, but Charlie Chaplin did not seem to do too badly out of it – by 1916, he was rumoured to be earning £2,000 a week. Another member of the troupe, Arthur Jefferson, would later follow him; but he would become better known as Stan Laurel, half of Laurel and Hardy.

British servicemen would also take the troupe's name with them into the trenches, in a bitterly ironic song:

We are Fred Karno's Army,
The ragtime infantry;
We cannot shoot, we cannot fight,
*What ****** use are we? . . .*

The gramophone – the must-have home entertainment system of the war years.

The
PANTOMIME AT HOME

as well as the Theatre-at-Home
——that's what you possess in a

'His Master's Voice'
GRAMOPHONE

with a set of the new Pantomime Records of the best hits including 'Sister Susie's Sewing Shirts for Soldiers,' 'We're Irish and proud of it too!' 'They sang 'God save the King,' 'Wonderful Rose of Love' and the exquisite 'Sunshine of your Smile' by Olga Elgar & Eli Hudson
Write for Coloured Folder to:
Gramophone Co Ltd : Hayes · Midd.

NEW · PANTOMIME · RECORDS

International diplomacy in 1914 may have been moving towards war, but the minutiae of everyday life continued to preoccupy people. The pre-war years had seen the emergence of the internal combustion engine, powering new modes of transport. The trend was not universally welcomed; and one of the unexpected places where this was so was on the River Thames, in the months immediately before the war:

> *A Taplow boat proprietor . . . interviewed by a press representative, gave it as his opinion that the popularity of the Thames was on the wane. The principal reason to which this doleful gentleman ascribes this state of affairs is that 'all the young sparks are on the road now. They've got their cars or motor bicycles, and they seem to like blazing along the road better than taking it easy in a punt' is his contention and it is not improbable that, at some of our riverside resorts, there may be something to be said for this view.*
>
> *Things are so bad . . . that I can't bear to walk up to the road and see all the motors going past. Why, there are even girls who'll hang on the back of a motor bike, instead of making themselves comfortable in one of my punts.*[12]

But it seems the war prompted a revival of interest in the riverside:

> *Seldom if ever has the River Thames been more popular than this year. Every available bungalow, houseboat or shanty has been taken, and in almost every river resort board and lodging is well-nigh unobtainable. The holidaymakers are for the most part, women and children. Many families, whose fathers are on active service, have taken up their abode by the riverside for the whole of the summer months, not a few being housed under canvas. Boatmen are doing a roaring trade at wartime prices. Until recently, wounded from military hospitals have been the frequent guests of the visitors, but in some districts of late, for some inconceivable reason, the river has been put out of bounds, and although the men may loiter and loll on the banks they must not enter any boat.*[13]

As for motorcyclists, the war dramatically changed their public image, according to this editorial:

> *One of the most striking things emphasised by the war has been the transformation of the motor cyclist from something like a pest into a national hero . . . The motor cycle may be described as the mosquito motor vehicle. Its high speed renders it eminently suitable for the conveyance of despatches and the owners of such machines who have volunteered for active service, and who have been drafted to the front are at last able to gratify the height of their ambitions. They can let their machines 'rip' and for the first time are able to ascertain exactly what speed can be knocked out of them inasmuch as speed limits are unknown . . . Their recklessness is appreciated; their desire to annihilate time and distance meets with official approbation.*[14]

One of the risks that all belligerent nations run is exposure to appalling jingoistic doggerel. Enter the Pangbourne Patriotic Poet, better known to her husband as Mrs L. Davies. She had come up with something entitled 'A Call to Arms'. The first verse should give you a flavour:

Up arm and out, brave Britain's sons,
With hearts true to the core,
Up arm and out with all despatch,
You're wanted at the war.
In days of old you never failed
To answer duty's call,
Up arm and out, lag not behind
You're wanted, one and all.[15]

There were a further nine verses, all of equal merit to the first. The *Berkshire Chronicle* felt obliged to print them all. This must have rather undermined Mrs Davies' plan, which was to sell copies of it at 3*d* a time, to raise money for the Belgian Relief Fund.

Cinemas did well during the war years. It was estimated that half the population were going to the cinema once a week by 1917; these establishments benefited from the restricted opening hours allowed to pubs, and even many of the soldiers at the front were treated to cinema shows. But it seemed that not all places of entertainment were having to fight off eager crowds:

The tightening of purse strings, consequent upon the war, is having its effect not only on the trade and commerce of the country but also, of course, upon amusements and sports . . . Therefore it is not surprising to learn from the current issue of The Stage *that correspondents in many towns report diminished attendances at theatres, music halls and picture houses. The last-named seem, however, to be the least affected and perhaps this is due largely to the display of films illustrative of warlike fact or fiction. Picture houses have in them the means of giving a summary in graphic form of the news of the day, and by doing so they may make themselves almost as necessary, though not as indispensable, as the newspaper. With regard to the music halls, the ease with which artistes can give 'turns' of a patriotic stamp helps to maintain their popularity. Theatres, however are not so favourably placed. Their arrangements have to be made weeks, and sometimes months ahead, and it is well nigh impossible for them to alter their arrangements at a moment's notice.*[16]

This company at least was trying to update its production *What ho, Tango!* to match the times:

It is full of bright and breezy humour. It is a revue of the conventional kind, but it is one where there is great scope for the inclusion of topical hits and of course the Germans feature rather largely as the butt of the comedians' wit and if their remarks are any criterion to the general being of the warlike Teuton, he must be a curious sort of fellow.[17]

The music halls nationally employed some 100,000 people and, as the war began to impact on them, they made arrangements to keep going at least on a temporary basis. Musicians took a cut in salary, and proprietors and artistes worked out an arrangement for sharing such income as a wartime audience could provide. Some music-hall stars became actively involved in the war effort. Harry Lauder was active in Army recruitment

NEW HUDSON MOTOR CYCLES

10 per cent. discount off all Models for Cash.

Lightweights from £28. 4-h.p. £59 10s.

6-h.p. Twin £75 12s.   Cycles from £5 19s. 6d.

Callas, Sons & May, Ltd., 68 to 76, Oxford St., READING.

The war transformed motorcyclists from noisy hooligans to courageous deliverers of military intelligence.

in 1914 and 1915. After his only son died on the Western Front in December 1916, he took to taking concert parties to the front line, to entertain the troops there.

In the Second World War, holiday rail travel was seriously constrained, with large parts of the coast off-limits to civilians and any leisure travel open to the question 'Is your journey really necessary?' Few such constraints seemed to apply to holiday travel in the Great War (try as the train companies might to discourage leisure travel), if this account of the 1918 August Bank Holiday is anything to go by:

The great rush to the sea began early this morning and some remarkable scenes

**For the first time, cinemas give the civilian population a taste
of life on the battlefield.**

*were witnessed at Victoria [Manchester] station. Blackpool will be the principal
destination of the trippers and the accommodation at this popular resort will
undoubtedly be heavily taxed. The Lancashire and Yorkshire Railway Company
have arranged for nineteen schedule [sic] trains today and a couple of days ago
the whole of the rationed bookings had been made. The tickets available for
tomorrow, despite the making of extra train provision, were nearly exhausted last
night.*

    *As early as seven o'clock this morning the pleasure seekers heavily laden with
luggage were waiting at Victoria station for the 8.45 train . . . The street boys
reaped a rich harvest carrying luggage to the station, but once at Victoria the
holidaymakers had perforce to struggle with their own boxes, for porters are at a
discount.*[18]

Accommodation was indeed at a premium at the resorts, and over the next few days the
press carried reports of holidaymakers sleeping on the beach, the promenade and, in one
case, in the recreation room of the local police station.

    One man who clearly did not wish to have his travel arrangements interrupted by the
holidaymaking masses introduced himself to railway officials at Crewe as the Prince of
Wales, and demanded a special train to be laid on, to take him to Perth. When this was
unsuccessful, he went to other officials with the story that he was the Chairman of both
the Great Northern and the London and North Western Railway Companies. Further
enquiries revealed that he was in fact an escapee from a private lunatic asylum in
Staffordshire, and the appropriate transport was indeed laid on for him.

Chapter 11
Victory and Beyond

As victory started to look ever more certain, people in the trenches and the munitions factories alike began to dream of the better world that would come with peace. Prime Minister Lloyd George promised homes fit for heroes and Reading's biggest employer, biscuit manufacturer Huntley and Palmer, announced plans to reduce the working week from 52 to 48 hours. For good measure, they would even give a week's holiday with pay to all employees with three years' service (and military service counted towards those three years). But there was still one piece of unfinished business to be completed.

Hang the Kaiser and make Germany pay!

Thoughts turned to the terms of the peace settlement. After such a war, it is perhaps no surprise that magnanimity did not feature large in the public's agenda, as this editorial suggests:

> *It is the great fear of the vast majority of the population that our Statesmen and those of our Allies will be cheated by words of the full victory that our arms have won . . . The instinct of us all is that our safety lies in no parlaying before the Armistice, the terms of which must make it impossible for Germany to resume the war. After that, as Lord Wrenbury says 'Let Hindenburg and Ludendorff publicly surrender their swords and the Allies occupy Berlin and Vienna'.[1]*

As for making Germany pay:

> *The central Empires must foot the bill [for the war] and among other things Germany must be made to hand over her merchant shipping to replace the ships sunk.[2]*

Armistice, peace, victory!

The first intimation newspaper readers may have had that peace was about to break out might have been this tiny piece of stop press, inserted somewhere in their local newspaper:

> *Thursday evening*

> *Reuters Agency is informed that, according to official American information, the Armistice with Germany was signed at 2.30 today.[3]*

In Henley, news of the Armistice first reached the town via a telegram from the *Daily Mail* to a local newsagent. He proudly displayed the telegram in his window and word spread like wildfire; hundreds of people flocked to queue up and read it. The Armistice came into effect from 11.00am on 11 November and communities up and down the country took to the streets to celebrate. Factory sirens, train whistles and church bells were all used to convey the good news. What follows is typical of the celebrations up and down the country:

The marvellous thing was the rapidity with which the flags made their appearance, alike on the business premises and in the possession of the drivers of vehicles and of pedestrians. They seemed to emerge as if by magic, and very quickly it seemed as if it were the exception for a person not to be carrying a flag.

All sorts of discordant musical instruments were soon brought into requisition, and the streets resounded with the din of whistles and trumpets and rattles, and indeed of 'any old thing' which could add to the general expression. Impromptu processions were speedily organised, and in these exhilarating touring parties soldiers, wounded and otherwise, appeared to take a conspicuous share . . . Officers were quite as eager to show their delight as the men, and there were some novel impromptu methods adopted of displaying pleasure. One officer was wearing a Ulhan's helmet and other trophies from the front were brought out to show that the Bosch was finally discomfited.

The heavy rain which fell did not damp the spirits of the demonstrators, though it threatened at one time to make the evening very uncomfortable. . . .

half a dozen men were sent out to clean the lamps in the centre of town. It was also arranged that the whole of the lamps in the centre of town should be lit . . . the shading of lights in shops and houses was also withdrawn . . . The increased illumination in the streets was greatly welcomed by the people.

Broad Street . . . was the venue of an impromptu but none the less effective firework display. It was amazing where all the squibs and rockets came from . . . A number of detonators soon found their way onto the tram lines in Broad Street.

A remarkable scene was witnessed in Flint Street, where a gang of German prisoners were engaged on brick loading and hauling. When the news came to them they cheered as frantically as the guard did who had charge of them.

We saw but one effigy of the Kaiser, on which was the wording 'The German madman run amok'. There was hooting for it wherever it was seen. It was burnt in St Mary's Butts.[4]

The influenza epidemic

Just as the carnage of the war was coming to an end, another killer began stalking the nation's population – the century's worst influenza epidemic was under way. It would take 150,000 lives in England and Wales and over 15 million worldwide.

Normal life was interrupted by it in all sorts of ways. Secondary schools and Sunday schools were closed, concerts and sporting events where large crowds might come into close proximity were cancelled. Post offices had difficulty maintaining deliveries, with a third or more of their staff off sick, businesses struggled to stay open and the armed forces put places of entertainment out of bounds to their men. Insurance companies also

Dislodge Influenza with Bovril

BRITISH TO THE BACKBONE

Bovril offers an improbable cure for influenza in the days when advertising standards did not count for too much.

complained that they were being overwhelmed with life insurance claims from flu victims. As for getting to see a doctor:

On Monday morning there was a queue at Dr. Fosbery's surgery on the Oxford Road which extended around the corner of Kensington Road. It must have measured at least seventy yards.[5]

The virus had unexpected consequences for this woman:

A woman named Trussle of Finch Buildings, who had been unwell for some time, and who was attacked from the beginning of last week with influenza, rose from her bed and fell on the outhouse below from which she rolled into the garden, and her fall being broken, she received no serious injury. She was rendered unconscious however and was badly bruised . . .[6]

The epidemic brought out some fairly futile attempts at self-medication, and not a little hypochondria:

There is a strong smell of eucalyptus, cinnamon and quinine in the streets and places of public assembly. All who are not confined to their homes by influenza are dosing themselves with preventatives. The person who sneezes is regarded as a danger to the public health, and anybody who coughs is in peril of being carried off to a sanatorium.[7]

The post-war world

Even in the midst of the war effort, some were thinking about the post-war world. Early in 1918, the formation of the Comrades of the Great War was announced. This was set up to promote comradeship among anyone who served in the war:

so that neither their efforts nor their interests shall be forgotten or neglected. Today, these men are fed, clothed, housed and paid; tomorrow they will be struggling in the whirlpool of civilian life and forced to fend entirely for themselves. Demobilisation will not only take the uniforms off millions of backs, but will mean a stupendous readjustment of industrial conditions. It is necessary to prepare for this time if the change is to be made smoothly and efficiently.[8]

What kind of place should the post-war world be? Socialist politician Lorenzo Quelch, speaking to his local trade-union club, had no doubts:

The wage-earning class had a better opportunity than ever before to reconstruct the industrial life of the nation in such a way as to secure for themselves a very much fuller, happier and freer life. The workers were as unprepared for peace as the nation had been unprepared for war, and unless there was a properly organised scheme of reconstruction launched at once when demobilisation actually took place they would be faced with grave difficulties and dangers, but such tyrannical government as that of the Bolsheviks was illogical and criminal. As a socialist, he believed in revolution such as would secure the emancipation of the industrial workers. But there was a right and a wrong way of proceeding . . . Social revolution in this country might be accomplished without any disorder or bloodshed if the people only used the political power they had at their disposal. But before they used that power they must make up their minds what they wanted. They should go step by step in the direction of the complete control of the industries . . . There was no reason why the national government should not make the mines, shipping, the railways and agriculture all national property.[9]

But Mr Quelch and his colleagues seemed to be precisely the types that the Church of England was worried about, after the war:

The Church must be placed in possession of a Central Fund if it is to save the nation's soul amidst the materialistic influences of industrial and commercial reconstruction.[10]

They launched a £5 million appeal, to enable them to strengthen Church schools around the country and swell the number of men taking up a religious vocation. That autumn, the local press were bombarded with advertisements, from which the following are taken:

For lack of a Central Fund, the philanthropic activities of the church and its alleviative agencies, and its social work, are starved. Devoted men and women gladly give their services, but they work with inadequate equipment, in ill-adapted buildings and for totally insufficient salaries. Clergy and church workers do not receive a living wage. Hampered, and sometimes almost literally starved, they struggle on . . . The idealism of the church schools is at the root of national character. The church school aims to produce good Christians and in the effort produces good citizens . . .

Millions of men will return from the war flushed with victory, welcomed with deserved acclaim, to enjoy well-earned rest on full pay. Money and praise will not refresh their souls. Freedom from the irk of military discipline will not preserve them amid temptations intensified by the very conditions of their release. They can only be protected by the inward and spiritual grace which the ministry of religion will supply.

Lord Milner (from April 1918 the Minister for War), addressing the speech-day audience at Shrewsbury School, had some views about the post-war world that were remarkable mainly for their vagueness:

The generation of boys to which they belonged had a job before them much bigger, much harder and entirely different from what confronted their fathers and elder brothers when they first crossed the threshold of manhood . . . He felt with absolute conviction that after the war it was going to be for us a new world with new and immense difficulties and problems, and that we should need all our strength to restart this country on lines that promised a worthy, not to say a glorious future. We simply could not go back to the old slipshod ways. We had learned too much in the school of bitter experience how slack, how inefficient, how self-indulgent we had been, and all its costly consequences in the hour of trial. But we had learned also how much more we were capable of when we were really put to it than we ever imagined before.[11]

After further intimations of doom and gloom, he concluded by calling for an end to class conflict and starvation wages (by means unspecified) and the introduction of peacetime national service.

Winston Churchill, opening a fete at Chelmsford, actively discouraged talk of what might happen after the war, for reasons which were equally vague:

After the war all sorts of bright prospects will be opened. When we have won the war there are any number of fine things which we can do, and all sorts of classes of people will be able to participate. An opportunity unique in history will be provided to us. There will be a chance of building up a broader, better organised society here at home and, rallying round it, binding to it by unbreakable ties.[12]

Industrialist Sir William Lever had a rather clearer (if equally wrong-headed) view of how class conflict might be overcome in post-war Britain:

The next generation of employees and workmen will be the men who are now fighting side by side in the trenches, and this comradeship will create, if it has not already done so, a feeling of brotherhood, love and respect between them. That will be an enormous gain. This comradeship will, I believe, have far-reaching and permanent economic effects.[13]

Homes fit for heroes

The housing part of the preparation for peace was left in the hands of the National Housing and Town Planning Council, who were holding a series of conferences up and down the country in the summer of 1918. The Government was urging local authorities to plan now, so that building could start as soon as hostilities ceased.

Lloyd George's promise of 'Homes fit for heroes' was on many people's minds, and as early as 1915 the local press in Manchester was discussing the abolition of slums. But this contributor to the debate seemed to imply that the slums were the fault of their occupants:

A slum is a low, dirty street in a large town occupied by a vagabond class . . . Two things create a slum, viz: (1) a low, dirty street and (2) a vagabond class. Displace both or either of these elements and the slum disappears. This must be so, for if the street disappears the vagabond class must go; and if the vagabond class is removed and in its place is substituted a well-to-do class, the street at once ceases to be a slum . . . Many persons jump to the hasty conclusion that the proper and only way to abolish slums is to demolish the houses in the street, without thinking of, or caring what the ultimate consequences might be . . . [but] . . . if the vagabond class is driven out of a slum he must pitch his tent in a more respectable place, which in time will become a slum, and so on ad infinitum, until the while town is demolished.

His solution to the problem?

Remove the vagrant class by reforming it and you get rid of a pest and preserve the houses with all the attending benefits.[14]

The newspaper revisited the issue of housing in Manchester in 1918, and in particular the question of who should deliver all the homes that were needed. Up until then, the public sector had played very little part in re-housing the thousands that had been displaced by public and private slum clearance programmes, and there appeared to be little consensus on it being their responsibility:

Many thousands of new houses, letting at rents of 5 shillings to 10 shillings, are urgently needed . . . The health and wellbeing of the people are detrimentally affected and so far no adequate and generally accepted remedy has been agreed upon, much less put into practice.

It may surely be taken for granted that neither the Manchester City Council nor adjoining councils will lightly take over the responsibility of housing the people. These bodies will require to be absolutely satisfied, first that the financial assistance to be received from the state is adequate and secondly that it is a duty that has devolved upon them because the natural and proper source of supply by private enterprise cannot be resuscitated and that the municipality remains, in real fact, the only possible source of supply.[15]

Jobs for women

What were the post-war prospects for women, who had made such great advances in the labour market during the war? This editorial coverage of a ministerial speech suggested that there was both bad news and good news for them (even if the good news seemed rather more speculative):

The Parliamentary Secretary to Munitions says that, if there be not work enough for everyone after the war, the women must stand aside and make room for the men who come back. And so say all of us! The men from the front must be in the front of the queues of civilians, whether it a question of work or pay, food or fuel. But Mr Kelloway went on to say that, after the first inevitable confusion of sorting and returning soldiers and prisoners, women would be 're-absorbed into industry' – that is to say, they will be wanted to work for making a new world after the war, just as they were wanted to work for victory . . . there will be any amount of work to be done, and the women will know much more about the various trades than they did in 1914. They will no longer be put off by croakers who say they are not strong enough or clever enough to do the work that lies to

THE *Studebaker* LANDAULET

Winter motoring

has a distinct charm, and for those who through reasons of health cannot experience this pleasure in an open car, there is no type of coachwork more suitable than the Landaulet. The Studebaker Landaulet combines the advantages of both types as it can be used as a closed or an open car. When closed, it affords all the comfort and protection desirable while travelling under varying climatic conditions. The coachwork is London-built and can be supplied on either the Studebaker "Four" or "Six" chassis. Only the very best materials are used in its construction. Painted in an attractive shade of dark green and the interior upholstered in Bedford cord. The driver's seat is finished in leather. Two extra folding seats are fitted, also an interior electric light. Clear running boards. Adjustable wind-screen, etc. We invite inspection. Call upon any of our dealers throughout the country, or if in London, at our Showrooms. A trial costs you nothing.

The equipment on both chassis includes Electric Self-starting and Dynamo Lighting Outfit, change speed and brake levers on right side of driver, metal side valances, domed wings, large brakes, oil pressure gauge and petrol indicator on dash,

| STUDEBAKER "FOUR" LANDAULET **£410** | 875 × 105 mm. tyres on "Four" and 920 × 120 mm. tyres on "Six," detachable rims and spare rim, electric lamps, motor driven horn, Stewart speedometer, jack, pump and kit of tools. | STUDEBAKER "SIX" LANDAULET **£480** |

Write for a copy of the STUDEBAKER PROOF BOOK, sent free on request.

STUDEBAKER, Ltd.,
Managing Director, EUSTACE H. WATSON.
117-123, GT. PORTLAND ST., LONDON. W.

Telegrams: "Studebaker, Wesdo, London."   Telephone: Mayfair 5104 (4 lines)

Imported cars were still readily available.

hand, because they will know that the munitions work or the office work or the van driving that they have just given up wanted brains or strength or both, and yet was not too much for them.[16]

One group who would be competing with women for jobs, and who faced particular difficulties, were the many men left disabled by the war:

In order to strengthen England's 'business army' an appointments department of the Ministry of labour has recently been formed to cope with the resettlement in civil life of wounded and invalided officers and to arrange courses of commercial training for them at universities and business houses.[17]

The dawn of mass motoring

The internal combustion engine really came of age in the First World War, and it led this correspondent to speculate on the future of motoring after the war:

When the war is over, I am pretty sure that we shall find that the idea of motoring is chiefly the prerogative of the rich will very speedily disappear. We shall find that the motor car will be much more in evidence than it ever has been, and the demand will be amongst all classes of the community. We only have to look at what has been accomplished in America to realise this . . .

After looking unfavourably at Britain's comparatively low car ownership, the correspondent continues:

There are some who would have us believe that the authorities in this country are entirely to blame for this state of affairs. Unfair taxation, both as regards the car and petrol, and repressive measures are held responsible . . . but a point of greater importance is the fact that our manufacturers have failed in a large measure to realise the needs of the people, and have concentrated on the production of a few expensive cars, rather than upon the production of a large number of low-priced cars.[18]

And finally

According to this piece of contemporary humour, at least one man knew what he intended to do, come the Armistice:

First conscientious objector: 'What are you going to do when the war is over?'

Second conscientious objector: 'Join the army'.[19]

Notes

Alderley and Wilmslow Advertiser and Guardian, East and Mid-Cheshire Gazette (AWA)

Berkshire Chronicle (BC)

East Grinstead Observer (EGO)

Evening Swindon Advertiser (ESA)

Hants and Berks Gazette (and *Middlesex and Surrey Journal*) (HBG)

Hampshire Chronicle, Southampton and Isle of Wight Courier and *General Advertiser for the South and West of England* (HC)

Henley and South Oxfordshire Standard (HS)

Liverpool Courier (LC)

Liverpool Echo (LE)

Liverpool Post and Mercury (LP)

Macclesfield Courier and Herald, Congleton Gazette, Stockport Express and *Cheshire General Advertiser* (MaC)

Manchester City News (MCN)

Manchester Courier (MC)

Manchester Evening Chronicle (MEC)

Manchester Evening Mail (MEM)

Manchester Guardian (MG)

Newbury Weekly News and *General Advertiser for South Berks, West Hants and East Wilts* (NWN)

North Wilts Herald, Cirencester Times, East Gloucestershire and Berkshire Advertiser (NWH)

Oxford Times (OT)

Portsmouth Evening News and *Southern Daily Mail* (PEN)

Reading Mercury, Oxford Gazette, Newbury Herald and *Berkshire County Paper* (RM)

Reading Standard, Berkshire Times and *South Oxfordshire Weekly News* (RS)

Stratford Express (SE)

Slough, Eton and Windsor Observer (SEWO)

Southend Standard and *Essex Weekly Advertiser* (SS)

Surrey Advertiser and County Times (SA)

Chapter 1

1. AWA, 3 July 1914.
2. AWA, 3 July 1914.
3. MC, 1 July 1914.
4. SEWO, 11 July 1914.
5. PEN, 29 July 1914.
6. LE, 3 August 1914.
7. MCN, 15 August 1914.
8. PEN, 8 August 1914.
9. PEN, 29 July 1914.
10. SEWO and elsewhere, 8 August 1914.
11. SEWO, 5 September 1914.
12. NWN, 6 August 1914.
13. AWA, 3 July 1914.
14. OT, 8 August 1914.
15. AWA, 14 August 1914.
16. MC 5, August 1914.
17. Bertrand Russell, letter to 'The Nation', 15 August 1914.
18. Advertisement in BC, 1 July 1914.
19. Advertisement in BC, 1 July 1914.
20. OT, 25 July 1914.
21. BC, 1 July 1914.
22. NWN, 23 July 1914.
23. SEWO, 25 July 1914.
24. HS, 7 August 1914.
25. HBG, 8 August 1914.
26. PEN, 4 August 1914.
27. ESA, 20 August 1914.
28. HS, 7 August 1914.
29. BC, 31 July 1914.
30. LE, 11 August 1914.
31. *Ibid.*
32. NWN, 13 August 1914.
33. PEN, 4 August 1914.
34. OT, 8 August 1914.
35. AWA, 7 August 1914.
36. HBG, 15 August 1914.

Chapter 2

1. MG, 11 September 1908.
2. Quoted in Neil Hanson, *First Blitz* (Doubleday, 2008), p. 25.
3. OT, 26 September 1914.
4. AWA, 3 July 1914.
5. BC, 29 December 1916.

6. HBG, 16 February 1918.
7. HS, 2 August 1918.
8. Quoted in Hanson, *First Blitz*, p. 84.
9. HS, 2 August 1918.
10. NWH, 5 February 1915.
11. ESA, 4 August 1914.
12. SS, 13 May 1915.
13. *Ibid*.
14. *Ibid*.
15. *Ibid*.
16. Quoted in Hanson, *First Blitz*, p. 41.
17. HC, 5 June 1915.
18. LC, 3 September 1914.
19. BC, 5 October 1917.
20. LC, 21 January 1915.
21. OT, 27 February 1915.
22. Quoted in Hanson, *First Blitz*, p. 107.
23. *The Times*, 15 June 1917.
24. LC, 4 September 1916.
25. *Ibid*.
26. HBG, 26 February 1916.
27. PEN, 8 August 1914.
28. BC, 7 April 1916 – quoting from *The Times*.
29. *Ibid*.
30. SS, 17 May 1915.
31. *Daily Mail*, 30 September 1917.
32. OT, 2 January 1915.
33. *The Times*, 9 July 1917.
34. PEN, 10 September 1914.
35. BC, 27 October 1916.
36. NWN, 10 February 1916.
37. BC, 11 February 1916.
38. Quoted in Hanson, *First Blitz*, p. 186.
39. AWA, 25 January 1918.
40. BC, 5 October 1917.
41. BC, 3 May 1918.
42. *Ibid*.
43. RS, 9 February 1918.
44. BC, 12 April 1918.
45. RS, 12 October 1918.
46. RS, 26 January 1918.

Chapter 3

1. Archibald Forbes (1838–1900) and William Howard Russell (1820–1907) were pioneering war correspondents of the latter part of the nineteenth century.
2. OT, 22 August 1914.
3. *Ibid.*
4. OT, 26 September 1914.
5. BC, 1 January 1915.
6. OT, 2 January 1914.
7. LC, 2 January 1915.
8. BC, 8 January 1915.
9. *Ibid.*
10. AWA, 8 January 1915.
11. HC, 23 January 1915.
12. LC, 2 January 1915.
13. SA, 19 September 1914.
14. BC, 8 January 1915.
15. BC, 15 January 1915.
16. BC, 14 July 1916.
17. HS, 13 November 1914.
18. SA, 19 September 1914.
19. HBG, 1 January 1916.
20. NWN, 5 April 1917.
21. LC, 7 May 1915.
22. BC, 5 March 1915.
23. BC, 25 September 1914.
24. BC, 12 May 1917.
25. BC, 4 June 1915.
26. OT, 5 September 1914.
27. BC, 7 December 1917.
28. ESA, 10 July 1916.
29. AWA, 22 January 1915. Jack Johnsons were the nickname for a type of German artillery shell, named after the world heavyweight boxing champion of the day.
30. SA, 20 February 1915.
31. SA, 12 September 1914.
32. HS, 9 October 1914.
33. BC, 26 November 1915.
34. NWN, 6 January 1916. Max Immelmann (the correspondent spelt his name wrongly) was one of Germany's leading fighter aces, with fifteen kills to his credit when he was himself shot down and killed in June 1916.
35. BC, 3 March 1916.
36. BC, 10 September 1915.
37. BC, 11 June 1915.
38. HS, 2 October 1914.
39. HS, 25 September 1914.
40. OT, 6 February 1915.
41. MEC, 3 October 1918.

42. ESA, 17 August 1914.
43. HBG, 22 August 1914.
44. Headlines to a report in the ESA, 3 July 1916.
45. PEN, 1 July 1916.
46. MCN, 8 July 1916.
47. *Ibid.*
48. HBG, 25 May 1918.

Chapter 4

1. BC, 28 August and 4 September 1914.
2. HBG, 8 January 1916.
3. BC, 7 August 1914.
4. *Ibid.*
5. HS, 4 September 1914.
6. *The Times*, 8 July 1915.
7. NWN, 3 September 1914.
8. MEM, 30 June 1915.
9. OT, 16 January 1915.
10. HBG, 8 January 1916.
11. *John Bull*, June 1915.
12. LC, 2 September 1916.
13. *Ibid.*
14. BC, 14 January 1916.
15. ESA, 11 July 1917.
16. BC, 4 June 1915.
17. AWA, 17 March 1916.
18. BC, 14 September 1917.
19. *Ibid.*
20. BC, 28 September 1917.
21. *Ibid.*
22. *Ibid.*

Chapter 5

1. MCN, 5 September 1914.
2. BC, 25 May 1917.
3. OT, 6 February 1915.
4. BC, 9 November 1914.
5. BC, 9 March 1917.
6. NWN, 26 April 1917.
7. BC, 27 July 1917.
8. BC, 1 March 1918.
9. BC, 21 December 1917.
10. AWA, 25 January 1918.
11. MCN, 19 January 1918.

12. AWA, 25 January 1918.
13. BC, 14 September 1917.
14. RS, 20 July 1918.
15. HBG, 2 March 1918.
16. BC, 6 April 1917.
17. RS, 23 February 1918.
18. OT, 15 August 1914.
19. BC, 9 March 1917.
20. RM, 9 February 1918.
21. BC, 2 November 1917.
22. BC, 2 August 1918.
23. Rationing jokes © 1918.

Chapter 6

1. MCN 25 July 1914.
2. MCN, 1 August 1914.
3. BC, 4 December 1914.
4. OT, 25 July 1914.
5. OT, 1 August 1914.
6. BC, 23 March 1917.
7. AWA, 11 September 1914.
8. AWA, 8 February 1918.
9. BC, 9 March 1917.
10. BC, 18 May 1917.
11. AWA, 26 January 1917.
12. RS, 5 January 1918.
13. AWA, 10 March 1916.
14. EGO, 17 June 1916.
15. AWA, 8 February 1918.
16. AWA, 12 January 1917.
17. PEN, 2 September 1914.
18. MEC, 2 August 1918.
19. OT, 27 March 1915.
20. SO, 1 April 1917.
21. SA, 12 September 1914.
22. MCN, 15 August 1914.
23. Letter to HC, 16 June 1917.
24. SA, 1 July 1916.
25. MaC, 2 March 1918.
26. BC, 9 July 1915.
27. *Ibid.*
28. BC, 7 January 1916.
29. AWA, 12 January 1917.
30. BC, 11 May 1917.

31. PEN, 12 September 1914.
32. AWA, 8 January 1915.
33. NWN, 8 November 1917.
34. MC, 3 August 1914.
35. AWA, 5 January 1917.

Chapter 7

1. AWA, 21 August 1914.
2. MCN, 10 July 1915.
3. ESA, 20 August 1914.
4. James Haywood, *Myths and Legends of the First World War* (Sutton, 2002), p. 14.
5. 9 August 1914.
6. Correspondent writing under the pen-name 'Amity', NWN, 13 August 1914.
7. ESA, 12 August 1914.
8. *The Times*, 25 August 1914.
9. BC, 21 May 1915.
10. BC, 2 April 1915.
11. BC, 4 June 1915.
12. MCN, 10 July 1915.
13. NWH, 1 January 1915.
14. HC, 2 January 1915.
15. SA, 8 July 1916.
16. HS, 7 August 1914.
17. SA, 5 September 1914.
18. NWN, 1 October 1914.
19. BC, 12 February 1915.
20. SA, 12 September 1914.

Chapter 8

1. NWN, 23–30 May 1918.
2. BC, 20 August 1915.
3. HBG, 11 March 1916.
4. SO, 8 April 1917.
5. SO, 15 April 1917.
6. NWN, 6 January 1916.
7. MCN, 12 January 1918.
8. BC, 23 April 1915.
9. BC, 9 July 1915.
10. SEWO, 8 July 1916.
11. BC, 27 September 1918.
12. BC, 4 October 1918.
13. LC, 15 January 1915.
14. OT, 22 August 1914.

15. BC, 18 February 1916.
16. HS, 7 August 1914.
17. BC, 5 July 1918.
18. BC, 16 August 1918.
19. LP, 4 July 1916.
20. NWN, 18 January 1917.
21. SE, January 1917.
22. AWA, 28 August 1914.
23. ESA, 24 August 1914.
24. BC, 6 August 1915.
25. NWN, 9 May 1918.
26. NWN, 23 May 1918.
27. NWN, 14 November 1918.
28. HS, 18 January 1918.
29. NWN, 7 February 1918.
30. BC, 9 October 1914.
31. ESA, 24 August 1914.

Chapter 9

1. BC, 13 October 1914.
2. BC, 30 October 1914.
3. HS, 3 November 1914.
4. AWA, 30 October 1914.
5. BC, 12 February 1915.
6. NWH, 29 January 1915.
7. HD, 21 October 1915.
8. Douglas Haig, 10 April 1915.
9. NWH, 12 February 1915.
10. LE, 27 July 1914.
11. BC, 7 May 1915.
12. Defence of the Realm Act regulations.
13. BC, 25 February 1916.
14. Evidence to the Royal Commission on Licensing, 29 April 1930.
15. RM, 19 January 1918.
16. AWA, 9 February 1917.
17. BC, 15 November 1918.
18. HC, 16 November 1918.

Chapter 10

1. BC, 11 September 1914.
2. LC, 1 September 1914.
3. LC, 3 September 1914.
4. SE, 2 December 1914.
5. PEN, 12 September 1914.
6. SA, 5 September 1914.

7. AWA, 14 August 1914.
8. *Athletic News*, 7 December 1914.
9. PEN, 12 September 1914.
10. OT, 26 September 1914.
11. HS, 15 March 1918.
12. BC, 31 July 1914.
13. HS, 11 August 1916.
14. NWH, 15 January 1915.
15. BC, 4 December 1914.
16. MCN, 15 August 1914.
17. ESA, 25 August 1914.
18. MEC, 2 August 1918.

Chapter 11

1. BC, 18 October 1918.
2. BC, 1 November 1918.
3. BC, 8 November 1918.
4. BC, 15 November 1918.
5. BC, 8 November 1918.
6. *Ibid*.
7. NWN, 31 October 1918.
8. BC, 4 January 1918.
9. RS, 16 November 1918.
10. Church of England Central Fund appeal advertisement, November 1918.
11. LP, 1 July 1916.
12. LC, 11 September 1916.
13. LC, 8 September 1916.
14. MCN, 7 August 1915.
15. MCN ,19 January 1918.
16. RS, 2 November 1918.
17. RS, 20 July 1918.
18. BC, 29 March 1918.
19. BC, 25 January 1918.

Bibliography

Alderley and Wilmslow Advertiser, 1914–18

Berkshire Chronicle, 1914–18

East Grinstead Observer, 1914–18

Evening Swindon Advertiser, 1914–18

Grant, R.G. (ed.), *1001 battles that changed the course of history*, Cassell, 2011

Hampshire Chronicle, 1914–18

Hanson, Neil, *First Blitz*, Doubleday, 2008

Hants and Berks Gazette, 1914–18

Haywood, James, *Myths and Legends of the First World War*, Sutton, 2002

Henley Standard, 1914–18

Hylton, Stuart, *A Reading Century*, Sutton, 1999

Hynes, Samuel, *A war imagined*, The Bodley Head, 1990

Jane's fighting aircraft of World War One, Jane's, 1919

Joll, James and Martel, Gordon, *The origins of the First World War*, Pearson, 2007

Liverpool Courier, 1914–18

Liverpool Echo, 1914–18

Liverpool Post and Mercury, 1914–18

Macclesfield Courier, 1914–18

Manchester City News, 1914–18

Manchester Courier, 1914–18

Manchester Evening Chronicle, 1914–18

Manchester Evening Mail, 1914–18

Manchester Guardian, 1914–18

Massie, Robert K., *Dreadnought: Britain, Germany and the coming of the Great War*, Cape, 1992

Monbauer, Annika, *The origins of the First World War*, Pearson Education, 2002

Index